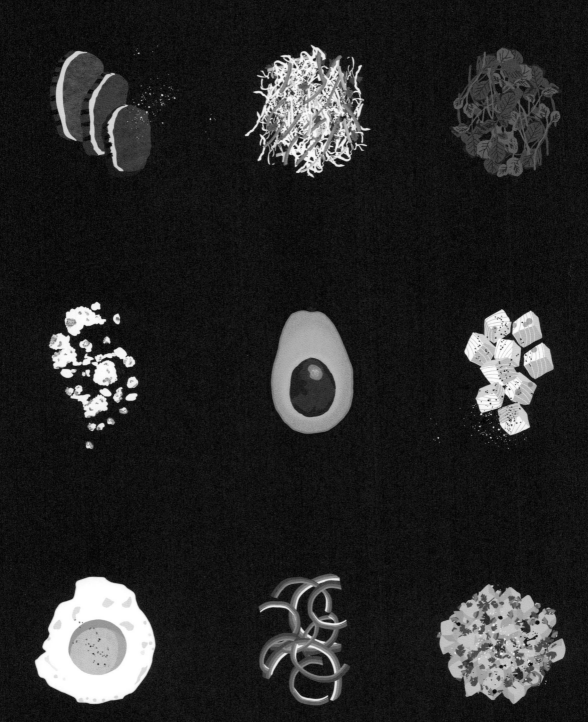

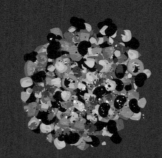

TACO-TOPIA

60+ MUNCH-TASTIC RECIPES

TACO-TOPIA

DEBORAH KALOPER

ILLUSTRATIONS BY ALICE OEHR

Smith Street Books

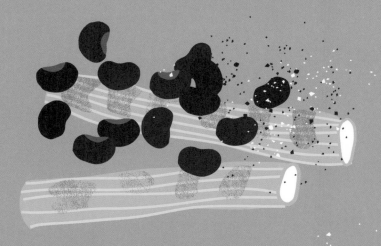

CONTENTS

INTRODUCTION...6

CHILLI ESSENTIALS...8

TORTILLAS, BEANS & EXTRAS...10

SALSAS, PICKLES & SAUCES...22

VEGETARIAN & VEGAN TACOS...38

FISH & SEAFOOD TACOS...52

CHICKEN & DUCK TACOS...66

PORK TACOS...80

BEEF TACOS...94

DRINKS...108

INDEX...130

INTRODUCTION

As far back as 3000 BC, the Aztecs in Mexico were transforming prized kernels of dried maize into a flat bread they called *tlaxcalli*. These were sometimes stuffed with other fillings, depending on what other ingredients were at hand — and so the humble taco was born.

Why and when the word *taco* came into being, remains uncertain. We do know that some millennia later, in the early 16th century, the notorious Spanish conquistador Hernán Cortés would arrange a taco feast in Mexico City for the captains under his command; they greatly admired this finger-licking finger food, as did the waves of Spanish colonists who followed. Around this time *tlaxcalli* was rechristened *tortilla* — by Cortés himself, according to some accounts — and a flour-based version was popularised when wheat was introduced from Spain. Despite these centuries of tumult, the spirit and soul of Mexico lives on in the taco's flavourful legacy.

Any North American state that shares a border with Mexico has an indelible link to its cuisine, giving rise to permutations such as the Californian burrito and the jalapeño-heavy cuisine known as Tex-Mex. But these days, big chain franchises sling uniform tacos to masses of college students throughout the US. Then there's the rise of upscale Mexican-fusion restaurants, serving trendy tacos and artisanal margaritas at staggering prices. Luckily street food trucks across the country, and the world over, persist in serving up simple taco dishes. These speak more truly of the taco's humble origins.

Versatility is the taco's biggest asset. They're breakfast, lunch or dinner (or perhaps all three). They can be eaten one handed, leaving the other hand free for a cold beer. Wherever you're ordering a taco, there's a guarantee of spiciness, crunchiness and glorious greasiness. It's the comfort food for everyone.

But the first thing you need to know is that all tacos start with a tortilla — a round flat bread, which can be made from either corn or flour. The two differ in taste and texture — flour tortillas have a more neutral flavour and are more pliable than their chewy corn cousins.

On the following pages you'll find a breakdown of the myriad chillies mentioned in this book. Then there are instructions on making homemade tortillas, as well as classic taco accoutrements — like refried beans, Mexican green quinoa, various salsas, guacamole and pico de gallo.

The chapters are then separated by your choice of base filling: vegetables and vegan-friendly tacos; fish and seafood; chicken and duck; pork; beef. Simple, right? Within these chapters you'll find traditional fare — such as baja fish (typical of the Tijuana coastline), and the beloved carnitas street tacos — as well as modern hybrids, featuring the flavours of a Louisiana Oyster Po' Boy, for example, or the crunch of Vietnamese pork belly banh mi.

Whether you're going for classic or swanky, the simplicity of any taco makes it a great all-rounder: a tasty snack, an ample meal, or the main event at your next informal dinner party.

Most importantly: freestyle it. When dressing each taco, follow your instinct and tastebuds, and don't worry too much about the ratios suggested. If you feel like an entire fistful of guacamole on your shredded brisket — do it. That's what tacos are all about. It's a choose-your-own-adventure story, where all roads lead to yum.

Oh — just one last thing... The entire taco ritual would be incomplete without a drink. So whether you feel like a refreshing fresca or spritzy michelada, you'll find those recipes at the end. *Salud!*

CHILLI ESSENTIALS

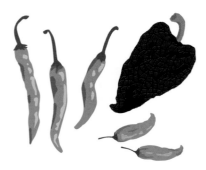

ANCHO

This large chilli pepper is the dried form of the poblano. The ancho's heat is very mild, allowing its plum, raisin and tobacco flavours to shine. They are heart-shaped and reddish brown to black in colour.

ARBOL

These are long, red, thin and shiny, with an intense heat similar to cayenne. The arbol chilli, also known as chile de àrbol, delivers an earthy burn. They are used in Mexican and Asian cuisine, and globally as a decorative garnish.

BIRD'S EYE

Commonly used in the Keralan region of southern India, and Thailand, these chillies have a tropical burst undercutting their powerful heat. They are named after a dubious likeness to a literal bird's eye, although they're sometimes known as Thai chillies.

CASCABEL

Small and cherry-shaped, the cascabel chilli is deep red when fresh and a dark brown when dried. In Spanish the name translates to 'little bell' or 'sleigh bell', a nod to its shape and the sound its loose seeds make when the dried chilli is shaken. It has a gentle spiciness, and when dried has an earthy, nutty and slightly smoky flavour.

CAYENNE

You can distinguish this pepper by its rippled skin and impressive length. The home cook may have only seen cayenne in its powdered form, but such powders are usually made with the hotter bird's eye chilli or a blend. Try and find the whole cayenne chilli to make use of its natural smokiness.

GUAJILLO

These are dried mirosol chillies. Shiny, and burgundy to brick red in colour, they have a sweet, moderate heat. They taste of fruit and berries with a note of smoky pine. In Central America, guajillo are typically used to flavour chicken-based dishes.

HABANERO

Originally from the depths of the Amazon, the habanero has spread far and wide. Its skin is thin and waxen. It's hot — very, very hot. As such, habaneros are adored by hot sauce fanatics. Habaneros are often confused with their Caribbean cousins, the Scotch bonnet, but do not share their sweetness.

JALAPEÑO

This chilli pepper is the most widely cultivated in Mexico, making up 30% of the country's chilli production. Typically picked before becoming ripe, jalapeño should remain green and have a moderate heat. They are commonly used in Tex-Mex and, considering their tolerable heat, make an ideal garnish. Chipotle are simply smoke-dried jalapeños.

MORITA

These dried jalapeños are smoked for a relatively short period of time to maintain a soft and silky texture. With a medium heat, morita have flavour notes of sweet red pepper, smoky chocolate, cherry and coffee.

PASILLA

Translating to 'little raisin', that's exactly how the pasilla chilli looks. It's the dried form of the chilaca chilli, with a mild heat and dark, wrinkled skin. The pasilla's herby aroma is contrasted by its licoricey flavour, making it perfect for use in mole sauces.

PEQUIN

These tiny chillies pack a huge punch, although a slightly smoky flavour should be detectable through their heat. Pequins are mostly used for pickling, salsas, soups and vinegars.

POBLANO

These large chillies can be eaten fresh. The poblano's flesh is mild with a slightly grassy flavour. The entire pepper can be stuffed fresh and roasted. When dried, poblano chillies are known as ancho chillies.

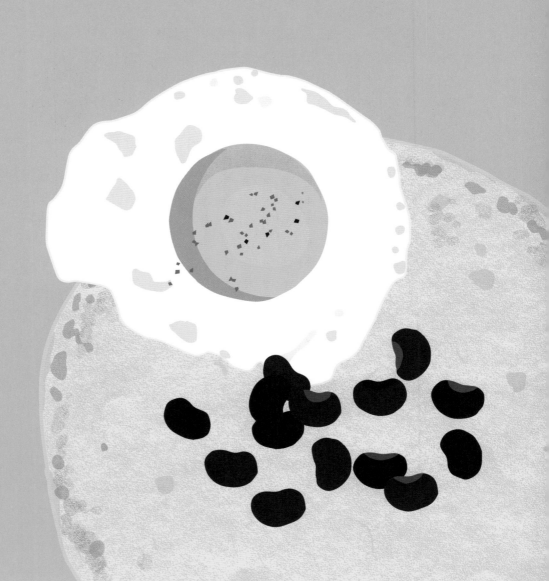

TORTILLAS, BEANS & EXTRAS

FLOUR TORTILLAS

MAKES 18 X 22 CM (8¾ INCH) TORTILLAS

600 g (1 lb 5 oz/4 cups) plain (all-purpose) flour

2 teaspoons fine sea salt

1¾ teaspoons baking powder

125 g (4½ oz) lard or butter, finely diced

330 ml (11 fl oz) warm water

Sift the flour, salt and baking powder together in a large bowl.

Add the diced lard and crumble it through the flour until the mixture becomes sand-like. Slowly add the water, little by little, while kneading the mixture together until it forms an elastic dough.

Divide into 18 equal portions, roll into balls, then cover with a cloth and leave to rest for 30 — 40 minutes.

Place a ball between two pieces of waxed paper and use a rolling pin to roll it out into a 22 cm (8¾ inch) round tortilla. Continue rolling out all of the tortillas, then cover with a cloth until ready to cook.

Heat a large flat cast-iron pan or chargrill pan over medium — high heat. Place a tortilla on the ungreased pan and cook for 1 — 1½ minutes on each side, until the tortilla is slightly dry to the touch, with lightly browned bubbles on the surface; it should feel dry, but still be soft and pliable.

While cooking the remaining tortillas, keep the cooked tortillas warm by stacking them on top of each other and covering them with a cloth.

Serve immediately.

NOTE

*For a fresh twist, try making **chilli flake** or **marigold petal tortillas**. While rolling out the tortillas, sprinkle the top of the dough with a pinch of chilli flakes, or edible flower petals, such as marigold.*

CORN TORTILLAS

MAKES 16 X 5 CM (2 INCH) TORTILLAS

220 g (8 oz/2 cups) masa harina (see Notes)

375 ml (12½ fl oz/1½ cups) warm water

2 teaspoons fine sea salt

Place all the ingredients in a large bowl and, using your hands, mix together until a dough forms. It should be pliable, almost like a play dough; add a little more water if it's a bit dry.

Knead the dough for 1 — 2 minutes, then divide into 16 equal portions. Roll into balls, then cover with a cloth and leave to rest for 20 — 30 minutes.

Place a ball between two pieces of waxed paper and use a rolling pin to roll it out into a 5 cm (2 inch) round tortilla. (If you have a tortilla press, place a piece of waxed paper on the base plate, then the dough ball in the centre, and another piece of waxed paper on top, then press the handle down to sandwich and flatten the dough into a tortilla.)

Continue rolling or pressing until all the balls have been flattened to size. Cover with a cloth until ready to cook.

Heat a large flat cast-iron pan or chargrill pan over medium — high heat. Place a tortilla on the ungreased pan. Flip after 10 seconds, cook for about 45 — 60 seconds, then flip again and cook for a further 35 — 50 seconds. The tortilla should feel dry, but not stiff or crumbly, and should be just lightly changed in colour.

While cooking the remaining tortillas, keep the cooked tortillas warm by stacking them on top of each other and covering them with a cloth.

Serve immediately.

NOTES

Masa harina (also known as 'masa de harina' or 'maseca') is a specialty corn flour available from Latin grocery stores and online. It is made with dried corn, which has been soaked and cooked in an alkaline solution, and is required to make tortillas.

*To make **beetroot (beet)** or **spinach** corn tortillas, replace 60 ml (2 fl oz/¼ cup) of the water with fresh beetroot juice or spinach juice, for a colourful twist.*

BEANS IN THE POT

SERVES 6 (ABOUT ½ CUP PER SERVE)

250 g (9 oz) dried pinto or black beans, soaked overnight in plenty of cold water

1 onion, diced

1 bay leaf

2 — 3 garlic cloves, peeled and smashed

1½ teaspoons dried epazote (see Note)

3 teaspoons sea salt

Drain the soaked beans and place in a large saucepan with the onion, bay leaf and garlic cloves. Cover with 7.5 — 10 cm (3 — 4 inches) fresh water and bring to the boil over high heat.

Reduce the heat and simmer, stirring occasionally, for 45 minutes to 1 hour, or until the beans are tender.

Stir in the epazote and salt and cook for a further 10 — 15 minutes, or until the beans are completely cooked through. Serve immediately.

NOTE

Epazote is a herb used in Mexican cuisine. It can be purchased from specialty grocery stores or online.

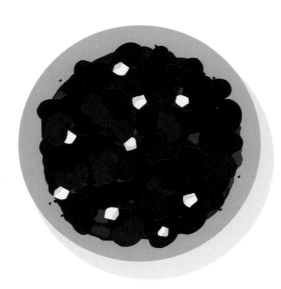

REFRIED BEANS

SERVES 6 (ABOUT ½ CUP PER SERVE)

80 ml (2½ fl oz/⅓ cup) vegetable oil or lard

1 small onion, peeled and halved

50 g (1¾ oz) piece of salted smoked pork (optional)

600 g (1 lb 5 oz/3½ cups) cooked pinto or black beans (see Note)

approximately 170 ml (5½ fl oz/⅔ cup) cooking liquid reserved from the beans, or chicken stock or water

TO SERVE

crumbled cheese, such as cotija, oaxaca, queso fresco, feta, mozzarella or ricotta

Warm the oil in a cast-iron pan over medium heat. Add the onion and smoked pork, if using. Heat through to flavour the oil for 1 — 2 minutes, then remove the onion and smoked pork and reserve for another use.

Add the beans and stir the flavoured oil through, then cook for about 5 — 8 minutes.

Smash the beans with a potato masher, or the back of a large spoon. Add the reserved bean cooking liquid or stock as needed, to achieve the desired consistency and creaminess, cooking for a further 4 — 5 minutes to warm the beans through.

Season to taste with sea salt and serve immediately, with a sprinkling of your favourite cheese.

NOTE

If cooking the beans from scratch, start with 250 g (9 oz) dried beans; soak them overnight and cook as directed for the Beans in the pot recipe opposite.

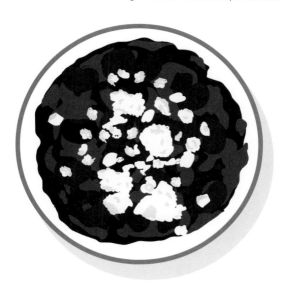

CHARRO BEANS (AKA COWBOY BEANS)

SERVES 6 — 8

2 teaspoons olive oil

180 g (6½ oz) Mexican chorizo sausages, removed from their casings

180 g (6½ oz) kaiserfleisch or smoked ham, cut into 1 cm (½ inch) dice

½ large onion, cut into 1 cm (½ inch) dice

2 fresh green jalapeño chillies, finely diced

2 — 3 large garlic cloves, crushed

1 tablespoon ground cumin

2 teaspoons dried epazote (see Note)

400 g (14 oz) tin chopped fire-roasted tomatoes

750 ml (25½ fl oz/3 cups) beef or chicken stock

1 bay leaf

1 kg (2 lb 3 oz/6 cups) cooked or tinned pinto beans

warm tortillas, to serve

Place a large saucepan over medium heat. Add the oil and sauté the chorizo and kaiserfleisch for 1 — 2 minutes, breaking up the sausage as it browns, then add the onion and cook for a further 3 — 4 minutes.

Add the chilli, garlic, cumin and epazote, stirring to combine. Stir in the tomatoes, stock and bay leaf and bring to the boil. Reduce the heat, add the beans and simmer for 15 — 20 minutes, to allow the flavours to combine.

Season to taste with sea salt and freshly cracked black pepper. Serve with warm tortillas.

NOTE

Epazote is a herb used in Mexican cuisine. It can be purchased from specialty grocery stores or online.

MEXICAN RED RICE

SERVES 6

60 ml (2 fl oz/¼ cup) olive oil

400 g (14 oz/2 cups) uncooked long-grain white rice

1 small onion, diced

1 small carrot, diced

1 large garlic clove, crushed

125 ml (4 fl oz/½ cup) tomato passata (puréed tomatoes)

750 ml (25½ fl oz/3 cups) chicken stock, vegetable stock or water

2 teaspoons fine sea salt

80 g (2¾ oz/½ cup) peas (blanched if fresh, thawed if frozen)

Warm the oil in a saucepan over medium heat. Add the rice and stir to coat the grains with the oil. Cook, stirring, for about 5—6 minutes.

Add the onion and carrot and cook for a further 5—6 minutes, then add the garlic and stir constantly for 1—2 minutes, until the onion is translucent and soft.

Add the passata, stock and salt, stirring to combine.

Bring to the boil, then reduce the heat, cover and simmer for 18—20 minutes, or until all the liquid has been absorbed and the rice is tender. Stir in the peas to warm through before serving.

CHICHARRONES

MAKES 250 G (9 OZ) / SERVES 4—6 AS A SNACK

500 g (1 lb 2 oz) pork skin, or pork crackling, scored and cut into 3 cm (1¼ inch) wide strips

1 tablespoon flaked sea salt

2 teaspoons chilli powder

vegetable oil, for deep-frying

Preheat the oven to 150°C (300°F).

Place the cut strips of pork skin, fat side down, on a wire rack set over a deep baking tray (to catch the melting fat). Transfer to the oven and bake for 1 hour.

Reduce the oven temperature to 120°C (250°F), or as low as it will go, and bake for a further 1½ hours to dry the pork skin out.

In a small bowl, combine the salt and chilli powder. Set aside.

In a large saucepan, heat enough oil for deep-frying to 180°C (350°F). Carefully fry the pork strips a few at a time, taking care as the hot oil may spit. Cook for 45—60 seconds, or until the pork strips puff up and are golden brown in colour.

Remove with a slotted spoon to a wire rack and dust with the chilli salt.

Serve immediately, or store in a clean airtight container at cool room temperature and use within 3—4 days.

MEXICAN GREEN QUINOA

SERVES 4—6

200 g (7 oz/1 cup) white quinoa, rinsed

45 g (1½ oz/1 cup) finely shredded baby spinach leaves

45 g (1½ oz/1 cup) finely shredded baby kale leaves

2 spring onions (scallions), thinly sliced

¼ cup finely shredded mint leaves

¼ cup chopped coriander (cilantro) leaves

1 fresh green jalapeño chilli, finely diced

30 g (1 oz/¼ cup) slivered pistachio nuts

30 g (1 oz/¼ cup) pepitas (pumpkin seeds)

60 ml (2 fl oz/¼ cup) extra virgin olive oil

juice and zest of 1 lemon

Rinse the quinoa and place in a saucepan. Pour in 500 ml (17 fl oz/2 cups) water and bring to the boil over high heat. Stir, reduce the heat to a simmer, then cover and cook for 12 minutes.

Remove from the heat and leave to sit with the lid on for a further 10 minutes.

Fluff the grains with a fork, then place in a large serving bowl and allow to cool sightly.

Add the remaining ingredients and season with sea salt and freshly cracked black pepper. Toss to combine, then serve.

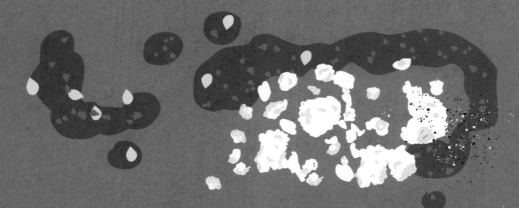

SALSAS, PICKLES & SAUCES

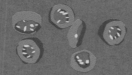

TOMATILLO SALSA VERDE

MAKES ABOUT 2½ CUPS

500 g (1 lb 2 oz) tomatillos, husks removed, rinsed

½ onion

3 garlic cloves

3 fresh green jalapeño chillies, stems and seeds removed

1 teaspoon sea salt

1 cup roughly chopped coriander (cilantro) leaves and stems

For a fresh salsa verde, roughly chop the tomatillos and onion and place in a food processor. Peel the garlic and add to the processor with the remaining ingredients and blend until well puréed.

For a roasted salsa verde, place the tomatillos, unpeeled onion and unpeeled garlic cloves on a baking tray. Cut the chillies in half and add to the tray, then place the tray under an oven grill (broiler) on high heat. Grill for 9 — 10 minutes, or until the ingredients are slightly charred and begin to blacken in spots, then turn them over and cook for a further 6 — 7 minutes, or until charred. Remove from the heat and leave to cool slightly. Peel the onion and garlic, then place in a food processor with the chillies. Add the remaining ingredients and blend until puréed. Use straight away, or cool before refrigerating.

The salsa verde can be refrigerated in a clean airtight container for 5 — 7 days.

ROASTED CORN & BLACK BEAN SALSA

MAKES ABOUT 3½ CUPS

2 corn cobs, husks and silks removed

125 g (4½ oz/¾ cup) cooked black beans

1 fresh green jalapeño chilli, finely diced; leave the seeds in if you like the heat

1 small red bird's eye chilli, seeds removed (optional), thinly sliced

½ red onion, finely diced

125 g (4½ oz) cherry tomatoes, quartered

¼ cup finely chopped coriander (cilantro) leaves

¼ cup finely chopped mint leaves

zest and juice of 1 large lime

1 tablespoon extra virgin olive oil

Place a chargrill pan over medium — high heat. Grill the corn cobs, turning on all sides, for about 7 — 10 minutes, or until slightly blackened and just cooked.

Allow to cool slightly, then carefully remove the kernels from the cob using a sharp knife.

Place all the ingredients in a bowl, toss to combine, and season with sea salt and freshly cracked black pepper to taste.

Refrigerate in a clean airtight container until required; the salsa is best served on the day it is made.

MANGO SALSA

MAKES ABOUT 2½ CUPS

1 large mango, peeled and stoned, flesh cut into 1 cm (½ inch) cubes

½ small red onion, diced

½ fresh green jalapeño chilli, finely diced; leave the seeds in if you like the heat

¼ cup chopped coriander (cilantro) leaves

zest and juice of 1 large lime

Place all the ingredients in a bowl and gently toss to combine.

Refrigerate in a clean airtight container until required; the salsa is best served on the day it is made.

AVOCADO TOMATILLO SAUCE (TAQUERIA STYLE)

MAKES ABOUT 2¼ CUPS

½ large avocado

½ quantity Tomatillo salsa verde (page 24)

80 ml (2½ fl oz/⅓ cup) lime juice

1 fresh green jalapeño chilli, roughly chopped; leave the seeds in if you like the heat

Place all the ingredients in a blender and purée until smooth. For a thinner sauce, blend in 1 — 2 tablespoons water.

The sauce can be refrigerated in a clean airtight container for 3 — 4 days.

NOTE

For a richer, creamier sauce, add 80 g (2¾ oz/⅓ cup) Mexican crema, sour cream or crème fraîche.

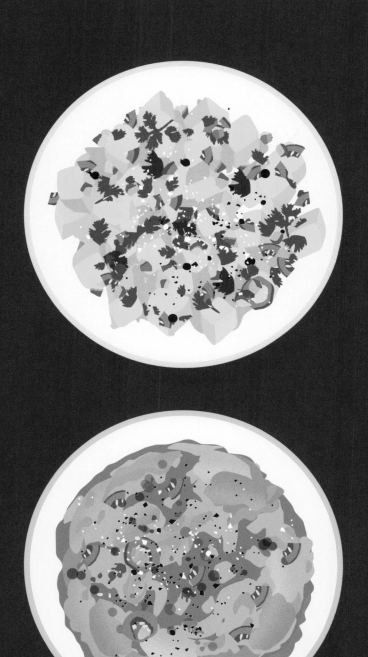

BLOW-YOUR-HEAD-OFF
HABANERO HOT SAUCE

MAKES 435 ML (15 FL OZ/1¾ CUPS)

125 ml (4 fl oz/½ cup) white vinegar

1 small carrot, grated

1 small onion, diced

2 roasted garlic cloves

80 g (2¾ oz/about 10) whole fresh habanero chillies, stems removed, seeds left in

1 ripe orange heirloom tomato

1½ teaspoons sea salt

1 teaspoon panela (see Note) or brown sugar

Place all the ingredients in a saucepan over medium heat. Stir in 125 ml (4 fl oz/½ cup) water and simmer for about 10 — 15 minutes, or until the chillies and onion are soft and cooked through.

Allow to cool, then purée in a high-speed blender for a smooth consistency.

The sauce will keep in the fridge for 5 — 7 days in a clean airtight container.

NOTE

Panela is an unrefined cane sugar, typically used in Latin American recipes.

RED TOMATO SALSA

MAKES ABOUT 2 CUPS

400 g (14 oz) ripe tomatoes, roughly chopped

1 fresh red jalapeño chilli, stem removed, seeds left in

½ small red onion, roughly chopped

2 garlic cloves, peeled

1 teaspoon sea salt

1½ tablespoons lime juice

¼ cup chopped coriander (cilantro) leaves

Place all the ingredients in a blender and blitz until coarsely chopped to a chunky consistency.

The salsa will keep in the fridge for 2 — 3 days in a clean airtight container.

ROASTED TOMATO SALSA

MAKES ABOUT 2 CUPS

400 g (14 oz) ripe tomatoes

1 fresh red jalapeño chilli, stem removed, seeds left in

½ small red onion, unpeeled

2 garlic cloves, unpeeled

1 teaspoon sea salt

1½ tablespoons lime juice

¼ cup chopped coriander (cilantro) leaves

Place a cast-iron pan or chargrill pan over high heat and add the tomatoes, chilli, onion half and garlic cloves. Roast the garlic for 6 — 7 minutes, and the tomatoes, chilli and onion for about 12 — 14 minutes, or until blackened, charred and softly roasted.

Allow to cool, then peel the garlic and add to a blender with all the remaining ingredients. Blitz until coarsely chopped, or to your liking. Taste and adjust the seasoning if desired.

The salsa will keep in the fridge for 2 — 3 days in a clean airtight container.

NOTE
If you're worried about the heat from the chilli, you can remove the seeds before blending the salsa, then gradually add them in to achieve the desired degree of heat.

PINEAPPLE SALSA

MAKES ABOUT 2½ CUPS

320 g (11½ oz/2 cups) chopped fresh pineapple, cut into 1 cm (½ inch) dice

¼ red onion, thinly sliced

1 fresh green jalapeño chilli, halved lengthways and thinly sliced; keep the seeds in if you like the heat

1 tablespoon chopped coriander (cilantro) leaves

1 tablespoon chopped mint leaves

zest and juice of 1 large lime

Combine all the ingredients in a bowl. Taste and adjust the lime juice to your liking, then season with sea salt and freshly cracked black pepper to taste.

The salsa will keep in the fridge for about 2 days in a clean airtight container.

NOTE

Instead of a jalapeño chilli, you could use 3 dried pequin chillies. First just dry-roast them in a pan, then grind them into a powder; you should end up with about ¼ teaspoon chilli powder.

RED CHILLI SAUCE

MAKES 250 ML (8½ FL OZ/1 CUP)

12 arbol chillies, stems and seeds removed; leave in some of the seeds for extra heat if desired

2 guajillo chillies, stems and seeds removed

2 large garlic cloves, unpeeled

1 large ripe heirloom tomato

30 ml (1 fl oz) white vinegar

1 teaspoon sea salt

Place a cast-iron pan or chargrill pan over medium — high heat. Dry-roast the chillies for 15 — 30 seconds, turning them so they don't burn.

Remove the chillies and place in a bowl, then cover with boiling water and leave to rehydrate for 20 minutes. Drain, reserving 30 ml (1 fl oz) of the chilli soaking water.

Meanwhile, dry-roast the garlic cloves and whole tomato for 5 — 10 minutes, turning occasionally, until the skins are lightly blackened and charred.

Peel the garlic cloves and add to a high-speed blender with the remaining ingredients, including the reserved chilli soaking water. Blitz to a purée.

The sauce will keep in the fridge for 5 — 7 days in a clean airtight container.

GREEN CHILLI SAUCE

MAKES 625 ML (21 FL OZ/2½ CUPS)

200 g (7 oz) fresh green jalapeño chillies, stems removed, roughly chopped

4 fresh green cayenne chillies

1 white onion, roughly chopped

1 cup roughly chopped coriander (cilantro) leaves

2 large garlic cloves, roughly chopped

125 ml (4 fl oz/½ cup) white vinegar

60 ml (2 fl oz/¼ cup) lime juice

2 tablespoons panela (see Notes) or brown sugar

2½ teaspoons sea salt

Place all the ingredients in a high-speed blender, add 80 ml (2½ fl oz/⅓ cup) water and purée until smooth.

The sauce will keep in the fridge for 3 — 4 days in a clean airtight container.

NOTES

Panela is an unrefined cane sugar, typically used in Latin American recipes. For a less acidic sauce with a milder flavour, heat 125 ml (4 fl oz/½ cup) vegetable oil in a saucepan over medium heat, then carefully add the raw green chilli sauce — it will spit! Cook for 4 — 5 minutes, then leave to cool. The sauce will keep for 5 — 7 days in the fridge.

GUACAMOLE

MAKES ABOUT 2½ CUPS

2 large ripe avocados, diced and mashed

¼ red onion, finely diced

2 tablespoons lime juice

½ fresh green jalapeño chilli, finely diced

2 tablespoons finely diced coriander (cilantro) leaves

fine sea salt, to taste

Place all the ingredients in a bowl and mix to combine.

Refrigerate in a clean airtight container until required; the guacamole is best served on the day it is made.

PICO DE GALLO

MAKES ABOUT 2½ CUPS

3 large ripe juicy tomatoes, diced

½ white onion, diced

1 fresh green jalapeño chilli, finely diced

1 small garlic clove, crushed

½ cup chopped coriander (cilantro) leaves

60 ml (2 fl oz/¼ cup) lime juice

Add all the ingredients to a bowl and mix until well combined. Season with sea salt and freshly cracked black pepper to taste.

The pico de gallo is best made near serving time, but will keep refrigerated in a clean airtight container for 1 day.

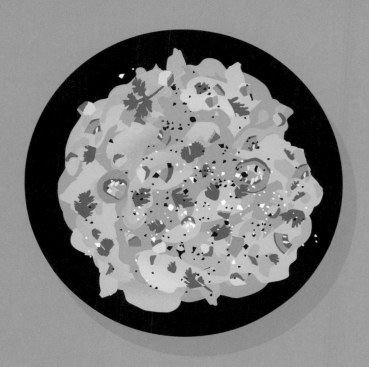

RED PICKLED ONION

MAKES ABOUT 3 CUPS

2 red onions, thinly sliced

2 garlic cloves, thinly sliced

2 red bird's eye chillies, split

2 allspice berries

1 bay leaf

¼ teaspoon black peppercorns

2 teaspoons sea salt

3 tablespoons white granulated sugar

250 ml (8½ fl oz/1 cup) apple cider vinegar

125 ml (4 fl oz/½ cup) lime juice

Place the onion slices in a heatproof bowl and cover with boiling water. Let sit for 20 — 30 seconds, then drain and refresh under cold water.

Place the onion slices in a large clean glass jar with the remaining ingredients, then seal and refrigerate.

The pickled onion will keep for up to 2 weeks in the fridge.

PICKLED TAQUERIA-STYLE VEGETABLES

MAKES ABOUT 3½ — 4 CUPS

1 carrot, sliced into coins

6 fresh green jalapeño chillies, halved, seeds removed

125 g (4½ oz/1 cup) small cauliflower florets

¼ white onion, sliced

6 radishes, quartered

250 ml (8½ fl oz/1 cup) white vinegar

1 bay leaf

½ teaspoon dried Mexican oregano (see Note)

¼ teaspoon black peppercorns

1 tablespoon sea salt

1 tablespoon white sugar

Combine all the ingredients in a saucepan over medium heat. Stir in 250 ml (8½ fl oz/1 cup) water and simmer for 10 — 12 minutes.

Allow to cool, then transfer to a large clean glass jar, seal and refrigerate.

The pickles will keep for up to 2 weeks in the fridge.

NOTE

Mexican oregano is related to lemon verbena, and has grassy, lime citrus notes. It can be bought online or from specialty Latin grocery stores.

VEGETARIAN & VEGAN TACOS

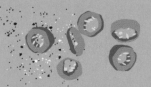

JACKFRUIT CHIPOTLE ADOBO TACOS

MAKES 12 TACOS / SERVES 6

2 x 565 g (1 lb 4 oz) tins jackfruit in brine, drained and rinsed (see Note)
1 tablespoon olive oil
1 brown onion, thinly sliced
4 garlic cloves, crushed
1 teaspoon each ground cumin, smoked paprika, ancho chilli powder and sea salt
½ teaspoon ground cinnamon
4 chipotle chillies in adobo sauce, plus 3 tablespoons of the sauce
400 g (14 oz) tin chopped tomatoes
250 ml (8½ fl oz/1 cup) vegetable stock
60 ml (2 fl oz/¼ cup) white vinegar
3 teaspoons brown sugar

VEGAN LIME CORIANDER CREMA

300 g (10½ oz) silken tofu, drained
45 ml (1½ fl oz) lime juice
3 teaspoons lime zest
1 tablespoon each olive oil and apple cider vinegar
1 teaspoon sea salt
½ teaspoon each chilli powder, garlic powder and onion powder
⅓ cup chopped coriander (cilantro)

TO SERVE

¼ white cabbage, shredded
12 warm Corn tortillas (page 15)
1 avocado, diced
coriander (cilantro) leaves
12 lime wedges
Mexican red rice (page 19)
Beans in the pot (page 16)

To make the crema, place all the ingredients in a blender and process until smooth. Taste and adjust the seasoning to your liking, adding more lime juice or chilli powder as desired. Refrigerate until required; the crema will keep in a clean airtight container in the fridge for 3 — 4 days, and makes about 375 g (12½ oz/1½ cups).

Place the drained jackfruit in a large bowl. Use your fingers to pull it apart and shred it into strands, then set aside.

Warm the oil in a large frying pan over medium heat. Sauté the onion for 4 — 5 minutes, then stir in the garlic and ground spices and sauté for a further 1 — 1½ minutes.

Add the remaining ingredients, along with the shredded jackfruit, stirring to combine. Reduce the heat to low and simmer slowly for 25 — 30 minutes, until the flavours are well combined and the sauce has thickened and reduced.

To serve, place some shredded cabbage on a warm tortilla, then top with some jackfruit mixture and avocado. Drizzle with some of the crema and garnish with coriander. Finish with a squeeze of lime and serve immediately, with rice and beans on the side.

NOTE
You'll need about 550 g (1 lb 3 oz) drained jackfruit.

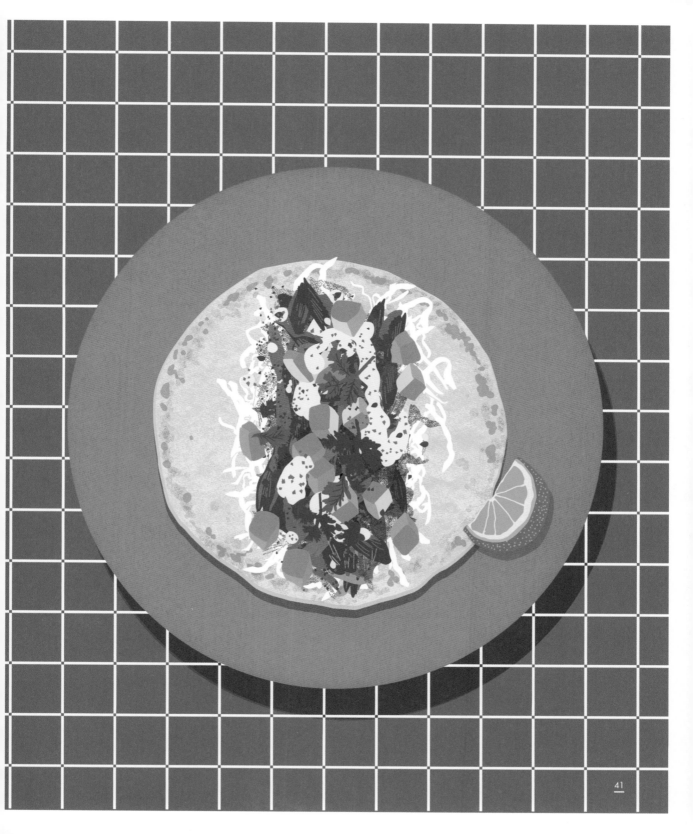

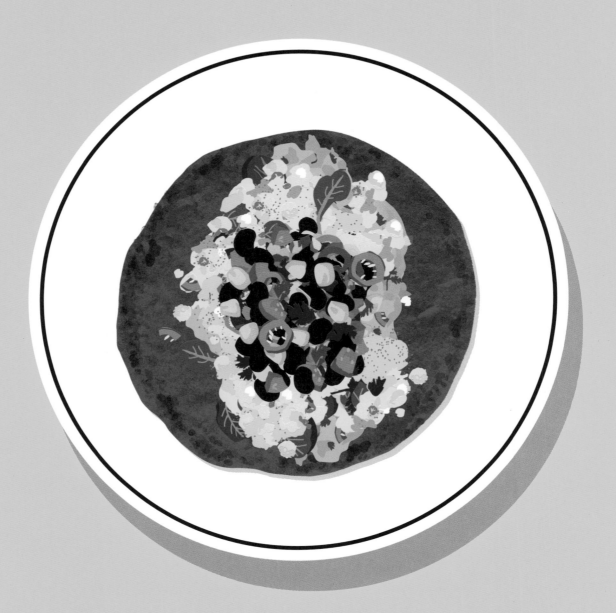

TURMERIC SCRAMBLED TOFU
& SPINACH TACOS

MAKES 12 TACOS / SERVES 4—6

2 tablespoons coconut oil

½ teaspoon ground turmeric

1½ teaspoons ground cumin

250 g (9 oz) firm tofu, well drained
(see Note) and crumbled

1 garlic clove, crushed

1 chipotle chilli in adobo sauce,
chopped, plus 2 tablespoons of
the sauce

90 g (3 oz/2 cups) chopped baby
spinach leaves

TO SERVE

12 warm Beetroot corn tortillas
(page 15)

Roasted corn & black bean salsa
(page 25)

Guacamole (page 34)

coriander (cilantro) leaves

Mexican red rice (page 19)

Warm the oil in a frying pan over medium heat. Add the turmeric, cumin, tofu and garlic and fry together for 1 — 2 minutes.

Add the chilli, adobo sauce, spinach and 60 ml (2 fl oz/¼ cup) water. Cook, stirring, for another few minutes, until the water has evaporated and the spinach has wilted through.

To serve, spoon some of the scrambled tofu onto a warm tortilla, then top with some salsa, guacamole and coriander. Serve immediately, with red rice.

NOTE
To drain the tofu, place it on top of several paper towels, place more paper towels on top, then weigh it down with a heavy plate and leave to drain. Squeeze out the water before using.

VEGAN NUTTY PICADILLO TACOS

MAKES 12 TACOS / SERVES 4—6

50 g (1¾ oz/½ cup) walnuts

80 g (2¾ oz/½ cup) blanched almonds

100 g (3½ oz/½ cup) cooked or tinned lentils

2 tablespoons olive oil

2 teaspoons tamari

2 tablespoons chopped coriander (cilantro)

1 teaspoon ground cumin

½ teaspoon ancho chilli powder

¼ teaspoon onion powder

¼ teaspoon garlic powder

¼ teaspoon fine sea salt

¼ teaspoon freshly cracked black pepper

TO SERVE

shredded iceberg lettuce

12 warm Corn tortillas (page 15)

shredded vegan cheese

Pico de gallo (page 34)

Avocado tomatillo sauce (page 26)

Place the walnuts and almonds in a blender and pulse into crumbs. Add the remaining ingredients and pulse to combine.

To serve, place some shredded lettuce on a warm tortilla, then add some of the nut mixture. Top with cheese and pico di gallo, drizzle with avocado tomatillo sauce and serve immediately.

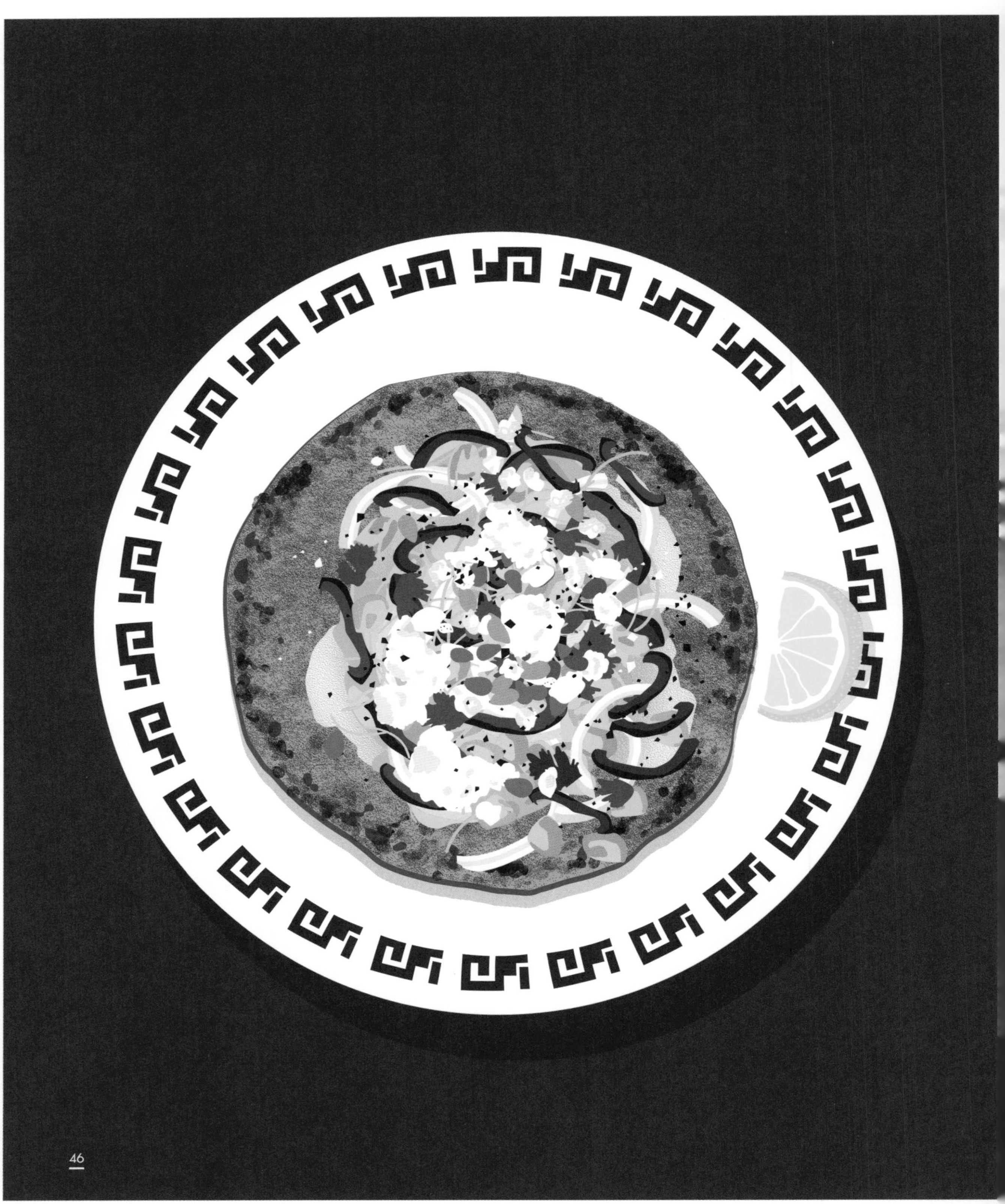

RAJAS POBLANAS & CORN TACOS

MAKES 12 TACOS / SERVES 4

300 g (10½ oz) fresh poblano chillies

2 tablespoons olive oil

1 tablespoon butter

1 brown onion, thinly sliced

300 g (10½ oz/1½ cups) fresh corn kernels

1 garlic clove, crushed

125 g (4½ oz/½ cup) Mexican crema, sour cream or crème fraîche

125 g (4½ oz/½ cup) queso requesón or ricotta

zest of 1 lemon

TO SERVE

12 warm Spinach corn tortillas (page 15)

cotija or goat's cheese

2½ tablespoons pepitas (pumpkin seeds), toasted

coriander (cilantro) leaves

12 lemon wedges

Beans in the pot (page 16)

Mexican green quinoa (page 21)

Heat an oven grill (broiler) to medium — high. Place the chillies on a baking tray and grill (broil) for 7 — 8 minutes on each side, until the skin has blackened and is charred in spots, and the flesh is soft. Place in a bowl and cover with plastic wrap. When cool enough to handle, remove the stems and seeds from the chillies, and peel off and discard the skin. Cut the chillies into thin strips and set aside.

Warm the oil and butter in a large frying pan over medium — high heat. When the butter has melted, sauté the onion for 4 minutes, then add the corn and sauté for a further 3 — 4 minutes. Finally, add the garlic and roasted chilli strips and sauté for 1 — 2 minutes.

Reduce the heat slightly, then stir in the crema, cheese and lemon zest until combined. Cook for 1 — 2 minutes, until warmed through and creamy. Season to taste with sea salt and freshly cracked black pepper.

To serve, spoon some of the corn mixture onto a warm tortilla. Crumble some cheese over, garnish with a sprinkling of pepitas and coriander, then finish with a squeeze of lemon. Serve immediately, with black beans and quinoa.

SAUTÉED MUSHROOM & ASHED GOAT'S CHEESE TACOS

MAKES 12 TACOS / SERVES 4—6

115 g (4 oz) butter
45 ml (1½ fl oz) olive oil
300 g (10½ oz) shiitake mushrooms,
or your favourite mushrooms, sliced
5 large garlic cloves, thinly sliced
1½ teaspoons chopped fresh thyme
½ teaspoon chopped fresh oregano
2½ tablespoons pine nuts, toasted
12 silverbeet or rainbow chard
leaves, about 180 g (6½ oz), shredded
zest and juice of 1 lemon

DUKKAH

50 g (1¾ oz/⅓ cup) almonds, toasted
2 tablespoons coriander seeds, toasted
2 tablespoons cumin seeds, toasted
2 teaspoons black cumin seeds, toasted
80 g (2¾ oz/½ cup) sesame seeds,
toasted
½ teaspoon freshly cracked black pepper
½ teaspoon fine sea salt

TO SERVE

12 warm Corn tortillas (page 15)
125 g (4½ oz) ashed goat's cheese
extra virgin olive oil, for drizzling
lemon zest
12 lemon wedges
Green chilli sauce (page 33) or
Roasted tomatillo salsa verde
(page 24)

To make the dukkah, place the almonds, coriander seeds and cumin seeds in a spice grinder and roughly blitz, or use a mortar and pestle to pound and roughly crush them together. Place in a bowl with the remaining ingredients and mix to combine. The dukkah will keep in a clean airtight container at cool room temperature for 3—4 weeks, and makes about 150 g (5½ oz/1¼ cups).

Warm the butter and oil in a large frying pan over medium—high heat. When the butter has melted, sauté the mushrooms for 1—2 minutes, then add the garlic, thyme and oregano and sauté for a further 1—2 minutes. Season with sea salt and freshly cracked black pepper. Add the pine nuts, tossing them through. Remove the mixture to a large bowl and keep warm.

Add the silverbeet to the same pan, stirring to coat in the remaining pan oil. Add the lemon zest and lemon juice, stirring for a minute or two until the silverbeet has just wilted. Fold the silverbeet through the mushroom mixture.

To serve, place some of the sautéed vegetable mixture on a warm tortilla. Crumble over some goat's cheese, drizzle with olive oil and sprinkle with a pinch of dukkah. Finish with some lemon zest, a squeeze of lemon and a splash of chilli sauce or salsa verde. Serve immediately.

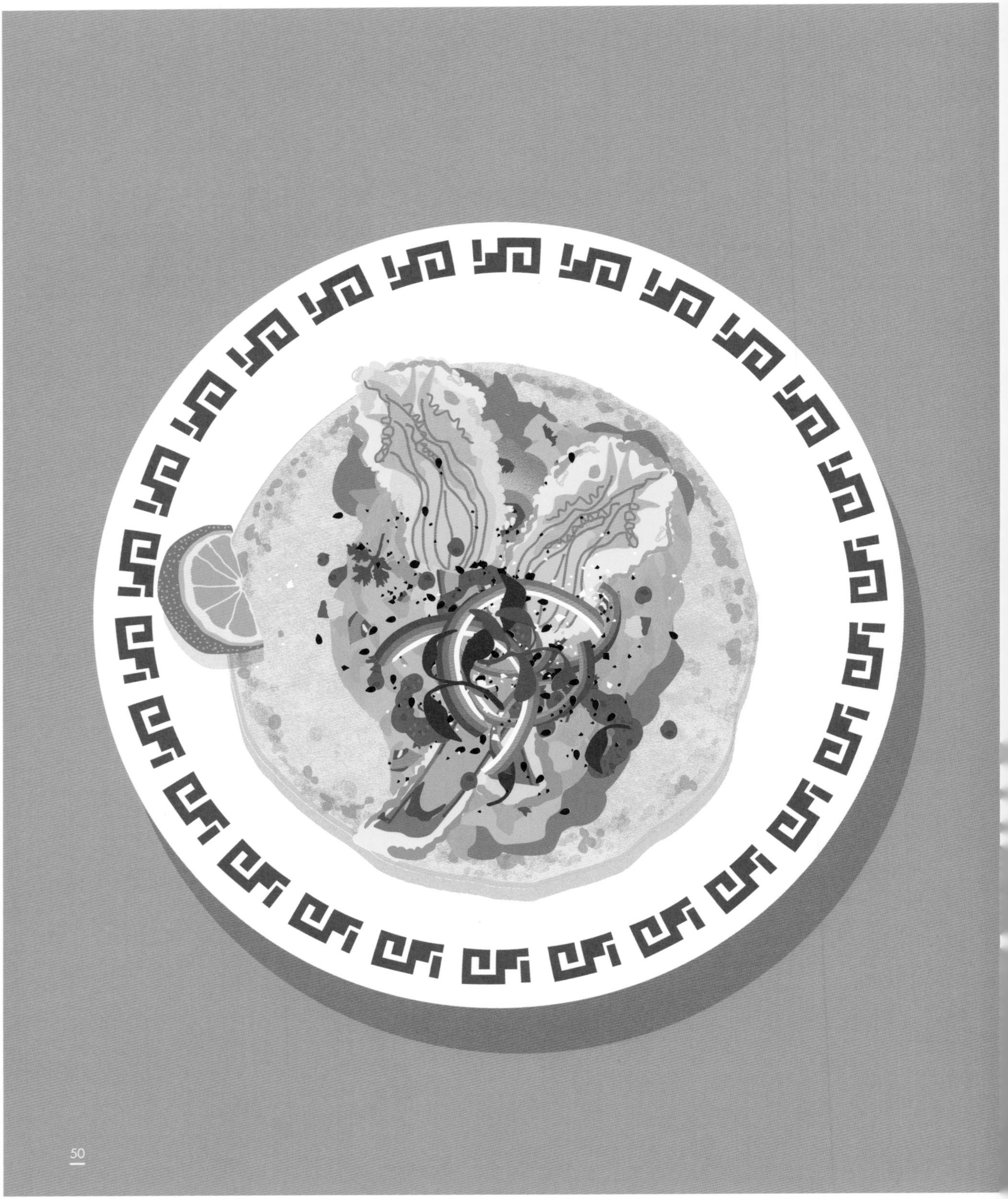

CHEESY DEEP-FRIED ZUCCHINI BLOSSOM TACOS

MAKES 12 TACOS / SERVES 6

12 baby zucchini (courgettes), with blossoms attached

125 g (4½ oz) oaxaca or mozzarella cheese, shredded

rice bran oil, for deep-frying

75 g (2¾ oz/½ cup) self-raising flour

¼ teaspoon cayenne pepper

¼ teaspoon chipotle chilli powder

¼ teaspoon fine sea salt

¼ teaspoon freshly cracked black pepper

250 ml (8½ fl oz/1 cup) dark Mexican beer

TO SERVE

Guacamole (page 34)

12 warm Corn tortillas (page 15)

Red pickled onion (page 36)

fresh green jalapeño chilli slices

1 tablespoon toasted black sesame seeds

coriander (cilantro) and radish micro-herbs

hot sauce (optional)

Gently open the zucchini flower petals, removing and discarding the stamens. Carefully stuff the flowers with a tablespoon of the cheese.

In a large saucepan, heat enough oil for deep-frying to 175°C (345°F) over medium — high heat.

In a bowl, combine the flour, spices, salt and pepper. Pour in the beer and whisk together.

Dip a few zucchini into the beer batter, then carefully add to the hot oil and cook for 3 — 4 minutes, or until golden brown. Drain on paper towel while cooking the remaining zucchini, and sprinkle with a little flaked sea salt.

To serve, spread some guacamole on a warm tortilla. Cut a zucchini (and its blossom) in half lengthways, and place on top of the guacamole. Top with pickled onion, jalapeño slices, and a sprinkling of sesame seeds and micro herbs. Serve immediately, with a dash of hot sauce, if desired.

NOTE

These tacos are also great served with Tomatillo salsa verde (page 24).

FISH & SEAFOOD TACOS

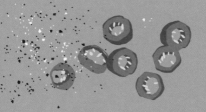

LOBSTER TAIL TACOS WITH LIME CHILLI BUTTER

MAKES 12 TACOS / SERVES 6

6 small lobster tails, each about 120 g (4½ oz) with shell, or 80 g (2¾ oz) flesh per tail, halved and cleaned

LIME CHILLI BUTTER

150 g (5½ oz) butter, melted

zest and juice of 2 limes

2 garlic cloves, peeled and finely grated

2 tablespoons finely chopped coriander (cilantro)

3 teaspoons finely chopped chives

½ teaspoon chipotle chilli powder

TO SERVE

12 warm Flour tortillas (page 12)

Mango salsa (page 26)

coriander (cilantro) leaves

12 lime wedges

Habenero hot sauce (page 28), optional

To make the lime chilli butter, place all the ingredients in a bowl and whisk to combine.

Heat a barbecue or chargrill over medium — high heat. Brush the flesh side of the lobster tails with the lime chilli butter, then place on the grill, cut side down. Cook for 2 — 3 minutes, or until the shells change colour.

Flip the tails over, brush on more lime chilli butter and cook for a further 2 — 3 minutes, or until the flesh turns opaque and is just cooked through.

To serve, remove the flesh from the shell, and place on a warm tortilla. Top with mango salsa, coriander, a squeeze of lime and a drizzle of the remaining lime chilli butter. Serve immediately, with a splash of habanero hot sauce if desired.

NOTE

These tacos are also delicious with Pineapple salsa (page 31), Roasted corn & black bean salsa (page 25) and Chipotle crema (page 104).

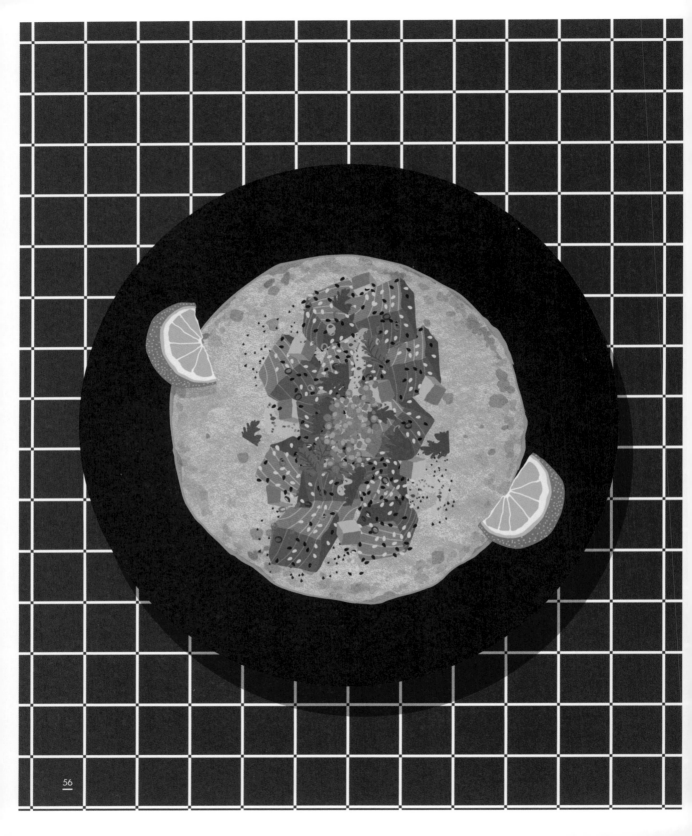

SPICY AHI POKE TACOS

MAKES 12 TACOS / SERVES 4

oil, for shallow frying

12 small Corn tortillas (page 15)

450 g (1 lb) sashimi-grade ahi tuna

1 Lebanese (short) cucumber, seeded

½ small sweet salad onion, peeled

1 avocado, peeled and stoned

1 teaspoon toasted black sesame seeds

1 teaspoon shichimi togarashi
(Japanese seven-spice)

SRIRACHA CREMA

125 g (4½ oz/½ cup) Mexican crema,
sour cream or crème fraîche

2 — 3 teaspoons sriracha sauce,
or more to taste

SHOYU & GINGER MARINADE

2 tablespoons shoyu

1 tablespoon rice wine vinegar

2 teaspoons toasted sesame oil

2 teaspoons honey

1½ teaspoons sriracha sauce

1½ teaspoons finely grated ginger

1 garlic clove, peeled and finely
grated

TO SERVE

tobiko (flying fish roe, available
from Asian grocery stores)

shichimi togarashi (Japanese
seven-spice)

coriander (cilantro) leaves

12 lime wedges

To make the sriracha crema, mix the ingredients together until well blended. Refrigerate in a clean airtight container until required. It will keep in the fridge for up to 5 days; makes about 125 g (4½ oz/½ cup).

To shallow fry the tortillas, pour vegetable oil into a wide frying pan, to a depth of 3 cm (1¼ inches). Place over medium — high heat, and heat the oil to 175°C (345°F). In batches, fry the tortillas for 1 — 2 minutes, until golden brown, then remove and drain on paper towel set over a wire cooling rack.

Cut the tuna, cucumber, onion and avocado into 1 cm (½ inch) dice and place in a large bowl. Sprinkle with the sesame seeds and shichimi togarashi.

In a separate bowl, whisk together the marinade ingredients, taste, and add more sriracha if desired. Pour over the tuna mixture and gently toss to combine.

To serve, place some poke mixture on a fried tortilla, drizzle with sriracha crema, then add a small spoonful of tobiko and a sprinkling of shichimi togarashi. Top with coriander and serve immediately, with a squeeze of lime.

OYSTER PO'BOY TACOS

MAKES 6 TACOS / SERVES 6

185 ml (6 fl oz/¾ cup) buttermilk
1 egg
60 ml (2 fl oz/¼ cup) hot sauce
1 teaspoon cayenne pepper
12 fresh oysters, shucked
oil, for deep-frying

SPICY REMOULADE SAUCE

160 g (5½ oz/⅔ cup) mayonnaise
2 tablespoons each dijon mustard,
freshly grated horseradish, chopped
parsley and lemon juice
3 teaspoons Red chilli sauce (page 32)
½ red capsicum (bell pepper), chopped
½ teaspoon each sea salt and pepper

SPICED PANKO CRUMBS

30 g (1 oz/½ cup) panko
35 g (1¼ oz/¼ cup) each cornmeal
and plain (all-purpose) flour
1½ teaspoons each cayenne pepper
and fine sea salt
½ teaspoon each chipotle chilli powder,
garlic powder and chopped oregano
1 teaspoon each onion powder,
hot paprika and black pepper

TO SERVE

6 warm Corn tortillas (page 15)
150 g (5½ oz/2 cups) shredded white
cabbage
1 spring onion (scallion), thinly sliced
garlic chives, finely chopped
2 teaspoons baby capers
6 lemon wedges

To make the spicy remoulade sauce, place all the ingredients
in a blender and blitz until smooth and creamy. Refrigerate in
a clean airtight container until required. The sauce will keep for
4 — 5 days in the fridge and makes about 125 g (4½ oz/½ cup).

In a bowl, whisk together the buttermilk, egg, hot sauce and
cayenne pepper until well combined. Add the oysters, then
cover and refrigerate for 20 — 30 minutes.

Place all the spiced panko crumbs ingredients in a bowl and stir
well to combine.

In a large saucepan, heat enough oil for deep-frying to 175°C
(345°F) over medium — high heat.

Remove the oysters from the buttermilk mixture, and toss to coat
completely in the spiced panko crumbs.

Carefully lower the oysters, in batches, into the hot oil and fry
for about 2 minutes, until golden brown and crispy. Remove and
drain on paper towel set over a wire rack, and sprinkle with
flaked sea salt and freshly cracked black pepper.

To serve, place some spicy remoulade on a warm tortilla, then
top with cabbage, spring onion and 2 oysters. Drizzle over some
more remoulade, then finish with a sprinkling of garlic chives,
baby capers and a squeeze of lemon. Serve immediately.

CEVICHE VERACRUZ TACOS

MAKES 12 TACOS / SERVES 4—6

600 g (1 lb 5 oz) kingfish fillet, skin and bones removed, cut into 1 cm (½ inch) dice

½ small red onion, finely diced

½ cup finely chopped coriander (cilantro) leaves

1—2 fresh green jalapeño chillies, seeds removed, finely diced

60 ml (2 fl oz/¼ cup) orange juice

125 ml (4 fl oz/½ cup) lime juice

vegetable or rice bran oil, for shallow frying

12 small Corn tortillas (page 15)

1 tomatillo, husks removed, then rinsed and diced

1 small tomato, diced

1 avocado, flesh cut into 1 cm (½ inch) dice

TO SERVE

40 g (1½ oz) watercress sprigs

4 heirloom or rainbow radishes, julienned

mint and coriander (cilantro) micro-herbs

extra virgin olive oil, for drizzling

Place the fish, onion, coriander, chilli and citrus juices in a glass bowl. Gently toss to combine, then cover and refrigerate for 1—2 hours.

To shallow fry the tortillas, pour vegetable oil into a wide frying pan to a depth of 3 cm (1¼ inches). Place over medium — high heat, and heat to 175°C (345°F). In batches, fry the tortillas for 1—2 minutes, until golden brown, then remove and drain on paper towel set over a wire cooling rack.

Remove the fish from the fridge. Add the tomatillo, tomato and avocado and gently toss through, then season with sea salt flakes and freshly cracked black pepper.

To serve, place some watercress on a fried tortilla, then add some fish ceviche. Finish with a little julienned radish, micro-herbs and a drizzle of olive oil. Serve immediately.

CHARGRILLED OCTOPUS TACOS

MAKES 18 TACOS / SERVES 6

2 bay leaves

½ teaspoon black peppercorns

1 onion, peeled and quartered

1 small orange, skin left on, cut into quarters

900 g (2 lb) octopus tentacles, cleaned

LEMON, CHILLI & GARLIC MARINADE

170 ml (5½ fl oz/⅔ cup) extra virgin olive oil

zest and juice of 2 lemons

⅔ cup finely chopped coriander (cilantro) leaves

2 — 3 bird's eye chillies, seeds removed, flesh crushed

5 — 6 large garlic cloves, crushed

TO SERVE

Guacamole (page 34)

18 warm Corn tortillas (page 15)

Red pickled onion (page 36)

1 fresh green jalapeño chilli, thinly sliced

coriander (cilantro) leaves

18 thin lemon wedges

Place a large saucepan of water over high heat. Add the bay leaves, peppercorns, and onion and orange quarters and bring to the boil. Add the octopus tentacles, bring up to the boil again, then reduce the heat to a simmer. Cover and braise for about 45 minutes, or until the octopus is tender when pierced with a knife.

While the octopus is braising, place the marinade ingredients in a large bowl and whisk to combine. Remove one-quarter of the marinade and set aside.

Allow the octopus to cool in the liquid, then remove to a chopping board. Cut the thickest part of the tentacles into 1.5 — 2 cm (½ — ¾ inch) dice. Leave the thinnest end of the tentacles in longer pieces, cutting them into 6 — 7.5 cm (2½ — 3 inch) lengths.

Add the octopus pieces to the marinade and toss to coat. Cover and leave to marinate for 35 — 45 minutes at cool room temperature.

To cook, simply barbecue over a hot chargrill for about 2 — 3 minutes, or until the skin begins to blacken and char, with the flesh remaining plump and juicy.

Place in a bowl and cover with the reserved marinade to soak up more flavour.

To serve, place some guacamole on a warm tortilla, then top with chargrilled octopus and some of the marinade oil. Add some pickled onion, jalapeño chilli, coriander and a squeeze of lemon and serve immediately.

NOTE
These tacos are also great with Pico de gallo (page 34), and Raw green chilli sauce (page 33) or Habanero hot sauce (page 28).

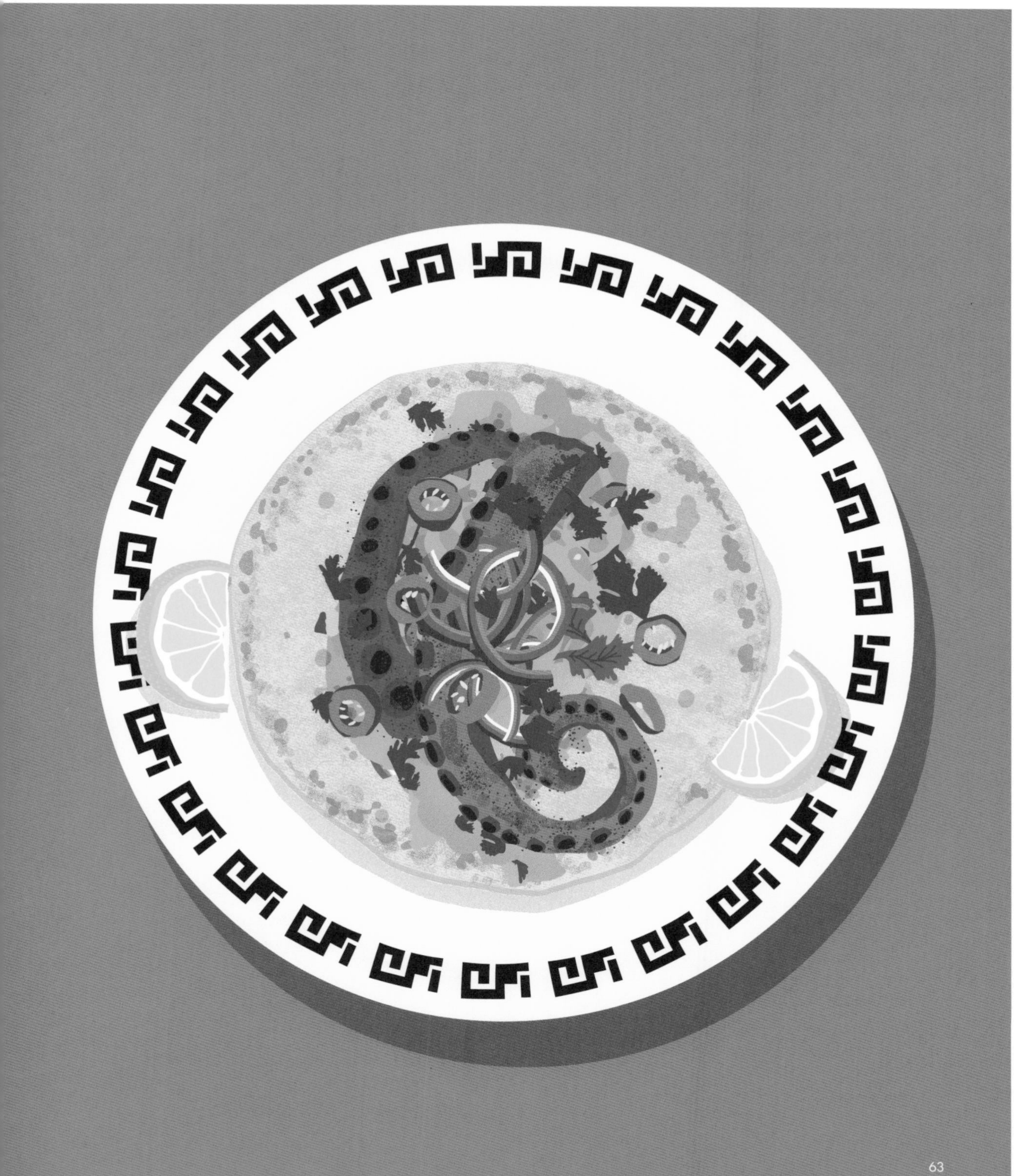

BAJA FISH TACOS

MAKES 12 TACOS / SERVES 4—6

oil, for deep-frying

225 g (8 oz/1½ cups) plain (all-purpose) flour

1 teaspoon chipotle chilli powder

1 teaspoon fine sea salt

½ teaspoon pepper

250 ml (8½ fl oz/1 cup) Mexican beer

900 g (2 lb) firm white fish fillets, such as flathead or snapper, skin and bones removed, cut into 24 pieces about 3 cm (1¼ inches) wide

CORIANDER SLAW

300 g (10½ oz/4 cups) shredded red cabbage

2 spring onions (scallions), thinly sliced

¼ cup chopped coriander (cilantro) leaves

60 g (2 oz/¼ cup) mayonnaise

60 g (2 oz/¼ cup) Mexican crema, sour cream or crème fraîche

zest and juice of 1 lime

TO SERVE

12 warm Corn tortillas (page 15)

Pico de gallo (page 34)

12 avocado slices

Chipotle crema (page 104)

3 radishes, thinly sliced

12 lime wedges

In a large saucepan, heat enough oil for deep-frying to 175°C (345°F).

Meanwhile, place 150 g (5½ oz/1 cup) of the flour in a large bowl. Mix the chilli powder, salt and pepper through, then whisk in the beer to combine.

Dust the fish in the remaining 75 g (2½ oz/½ cup) of flour.

Dip the fish into the beer batter, one piece at a time, and carefully place it into the hot oil. Fry 2—3 pieces at a time, for about 2 minutes per side, or until golden brown, crispy and cooked through. Remove and drain on paper towel set over a wire rack and sprinkle with flaked sea salt.

Place all the coriander slaw ingredients in a bowl and toss to combine. Season with salt and pepper to taste.

To serve, place some slaw on a warm tortilla, and top with pico de gallo and an avocado slice. Add two pieces of fried fish and drizzle over some chipotle crema. Finish with a few slices of radish and a squeeze of lime. Serve immediately.

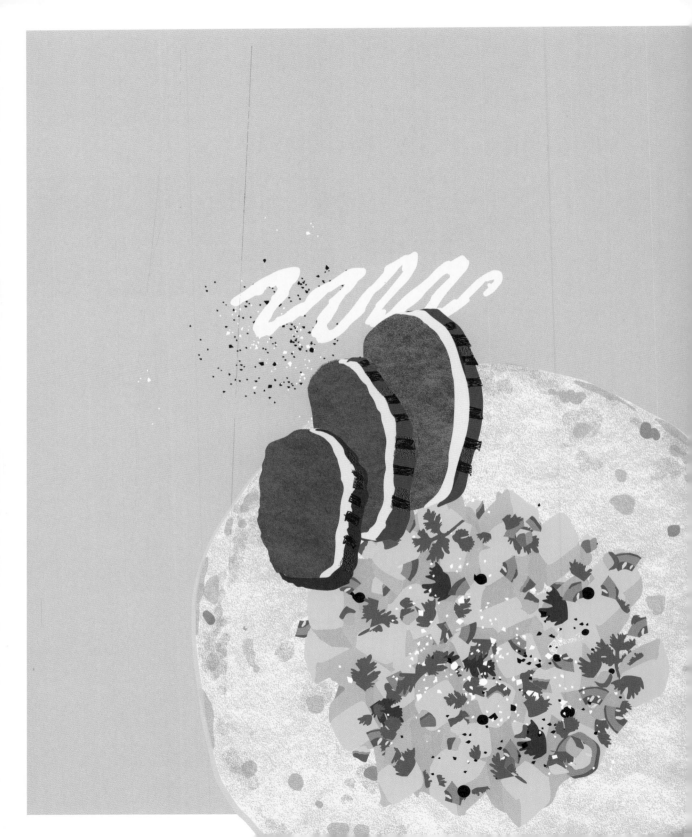

CHICKEN
& DUCK
TACOS

CHICKEN TAQUITOS

MAKES 12 TAQUITOS / SERVES 4—6

4 boneless chicken breasts, about
1 kg (2 lb 3 oz), skin removed

1 bay leaf

1 garlic clove, peeled and smashed

12 warm Corn tortillas (page 15)

vegetable or rice bran oil, for shallow
frying

TO SERVE

shredded iceberg lettuce

Avocado tomatillo sauce (page 26)

Mexican crema, sour cream or
crème fraîche

crumbled cotija cheese or mild feta

coriander (cilantro) leaves

12 lime wedges

Place the chicken breasts in a saucepan with the bay leaf and
garlic clove, then cover with cold water. Place over high heat,
bring to the boil, and cook for 1 minute. Cover with a tight-fitting
lid and turn off the heat, then leave to sit and slowly poach for
15—20 minutes. Remove from the heat.

Preheat the oven to very low.

When the chicken is cool enough to handle, shred the meat and
season with sea salt and freshly cracked black pepper.

Fill a tortilla with a small amount of the shredded chicken, then
roll up tightly and secure with a wooden toothpick to keep the
chicken enclosed. Repeat until all the tortillas have been filled.

Pour vegetable oil into a wide frying pan to a depth of 3 cm
(1¼ inches). Place over medium—high heat, and heat to 175°C
(345°F). Fry the taquitos in batches, turning now and then, for
about 2—3 minutes, until golden brown and crispy on all sides.
Remove to a wire rack set over a baking tray, and keep warm in
the oven while frying the remaining taquitos.

To serve, place some shredded lettuce on a plate, then top with
two or three taquitos. Drizzle with avocado tomatillo sauce and
crema. Sprinkle with cheese, coriander and a squeeze of lime
and serve immediately.

CHICKEN TINGA TACOS

MAKES 12 TACOS / SERVES 4—6

4 boneless chicken breasts, about
1 kg (2 lb 3 oz), skin removed

1 bay leaf

1 garlic clove, peeled and smashed

TINGA SAUCE

2 teaspoons olive oil

1 large brown onion, diced

2 large garlic cloves, crushed

1 teaspoon dried Mexican oregano
(see Note)

1 teaspoon ground cumin

2 x 400 g (14 oz) tins diced tomatoes

60 ml (2 fl oz/¼ cup) reserved chicken
poaching liquid or chicken stock

4 chipotle chillies in adobo sauce,
finely chopped, plus 2 tablespoons
of the sauce

TO SERVE

Mexican crema, sour cream or
crème fraîche

12 warm Corn tortillas (page 15)

crumbled queso añejo or feta cheese

3 radishes, thinly sliced

Red pickled onion (page 36)

fresh green jalapeño chilli slices

12 lime wedges

Place the chicken breasts in a saucepan with the bay leaf and garlic clove, then cover with cold water. Place over high heat, bring to the boil, and cook for 1 minute. Cover with a tight-fitting lid and turn off the heat, then leave to sit and slowly poach for 15—20 minutes. Remove from the heat.

When cool enough to handle, reserve 60 ml (2 fl oz/¼ cup) of the chicken poaching liquid for the tinga sauce. Thinly shred the chicken and set aside.

To make the tinga sauce, place the oil in a saucepan over medium heat, add the onion and sauté for 5—7 minutes, or until translucent and soft. Add the garlic, oregano and cumin and fry for a further minute. Stir in the reserved chicken stock, along with the tomatoes, chipotle chilli and adobo sauce. Add the shredded chicken and simmer for 8—10 minutes, or until the sauce has reduced slightly. Season with sea salt and freshly cracked black pepper to taste.

To serve, drizzle some crema on a warm tortilla, then top with chicken tinga, cheese, radish and pickled onion. Finish with a few jalapeño chilli slices and a squeeze of lime. Serve immediately.

NOTE

Mexican oregano is related to lemon verbena, and has grassy, lime citrus notes. It can be bought online or from specialty Latin grocery stores.

DUCK TACOS WITH CHERRY & BLOOD ORANGE SALSA

MAKES 8 TACOS / SERVES 4

4 boneless duck breasts, skin on and scored

CHERRY & BLOOD ORANGE SALSA

1 tablespoon diced French shallot

180 g (6½ oz) fresh cherries, pitted and sliced

125 ml (4 fl oz/½ cup) blood orange juice

60 ml (2 fl oz/¼ cup) Cointreau or other orange-flavoured liqueur

1 bay leaf

⅛ teaspoon white peppercorns, crushed

2 large blood oranges, segmented

TO SERVE

rocket (arugula) leaves

8 warm Corn tortillas (page 15)

Red pickled onion (page 36)

fresh coriander (cilantro) leaves

Habanero hot sauce (page 28)

Preheat the oven to 190°C (375°F).

Rinse the duck breasts, pat dry and season with sea salt and freshly cracked black pepper.

Place the duck breasts, skin side down, in a large ovenproof frying pan over medium heat. Cook for 2 — 3 minutes, until most of the fat has rendered out into the pan, then increase the heat and cook for a further 2 — 3 minutes, until the skin is crisp and golden brown.

Turn the duck over and cook for a further 2 — 3 minutes, then transfer the pan to the oven and bake for 7 — 8 minutes, to cook the duck through to medium.

Remove from the oven, keep warm and leave to rest for about 5 minutes.

To make the salsa, pour off most of the fat from the pan, then place back over medium heat. Add the shallot, cherries and orange juice and cook for 2 — 3 minutes. Stir in the Cointreau, bay leaf and crushed peppercorns and cook for 2 — 3 minutes, or until the sauce has reduced slightly. Remove from the heat and toss the orange segments through.

To serve, cut the duck breasts into 5 mm (¼ inch) thick slices. Place some rocket on a warm tortilla, then top with sliced duck and the salsa. Finish with some pickled onion, coriander and habanero hot sauce. Serve immediately.

NOTE

Instead of the cherry and blood orange salsa, these tacos are also great with Mango salsa (page 26) or Pineapple salsa (page 31).

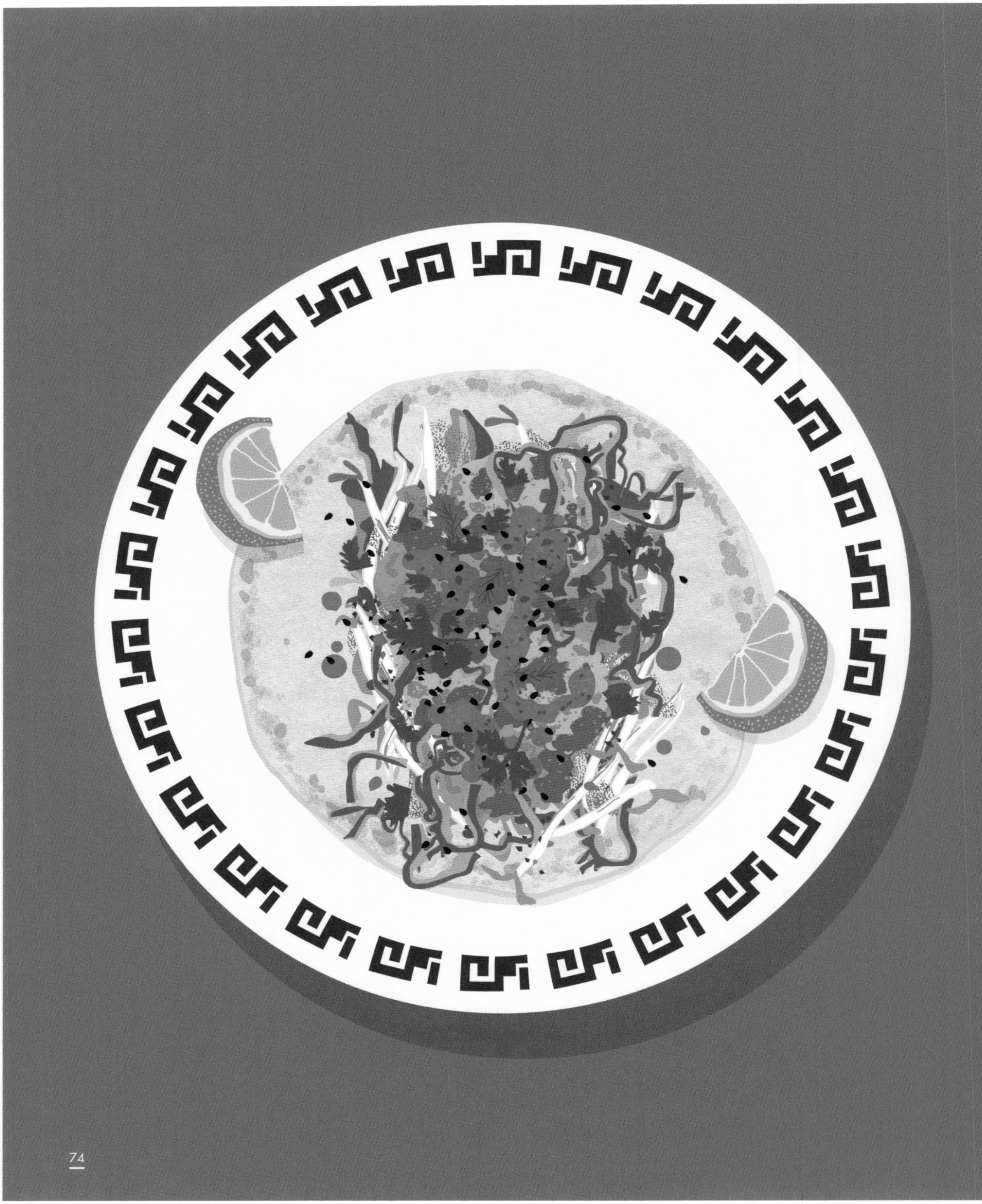

CHICKEN KARAAGE TACOS

MAKES 8 TACOS / SERVES 4

4 boneless chicken thighs, skin on, cut into 5 cm (2 inch) pieces

160 g (5½ oz/1 cup) potato starch

½ teaspoon sea salt

½ teaspoon freshly cracked black pepper

vegetable or rice bran oil, for deep-frying

TAMARI & GINGER MARINADE

4 garlic cloves, finely grated

20 g (¾ oz) piece of ginger, peeled and finely grated

60 ml (2 fl oz/¼ cup) tamari

60 ml (2 fl oz/¼ cup) sweet sake

2 teaspoons toasted sesame oil

1 teaspoon sriracha sauce

½ teaspoon shichimi togarashi (Japanese seven-spice)

SPICY SLAW

150 g (5½ oz/2 cups) shredded red cabbage

90 g (3 oz/1 cup) bean shoots

60 ml (2 fl oz/¼ cup) kewpie mayonnaise

1 tablespoon sweet chilli sauce

TO SERVE

8 warm Corn tortillas (page 15)

sriracha sauce

coriander (cilantro) leaves

1 teaspoon toasted black sesame seeds

Place all the marinade ingredients in a bowl and whisk to combine. Add the chicken and mix well, then cover and refrigerate for 30 minutes.

To make the slaw, combine all the ingredients in a mixing bowl and toss to combine. Cover and refrigerate until required.

Combine the potato starch, salt and pepper in a bowl. Remove the chicken from the fridge; drain and discard the marinade.

In a large saucepan, heat enough oil for deep-frying to 170°C (340°F). Toss the chicken in the potato starch, coating thoroughly. Fry in batches for 3 minutes, or until just cooked through, then drain on a wire rack.

Increase the heat to 190°C (375°F). Fry the chicken again, in batches, for 30—60 seconds, or until golden brown.

To serve, place some slaw on a warm tortilla and top with a few pieces of chicken. Serve immediately, drizzled with sriracha, and garnished with coriander and sesame seeds.

CHICKEN FAJITAS TACOS

MAKES 12 TACOS / SERVES 4

3 boneless chicken breasts, about 750 g (1 lb 11 oz), skin removed

1 red capsicum (bell pepper), sliced

1 yellow capsicum (bell pepper), sliced

1 large red onion, sliced

LIME, CORIANDER & CHILLI MARINADE

½ cup chopped coriander (cilantro)

125 ml (4 fl oz/½ cup) olive oil

60 ml (2 fl oz/¼ cup) lime juice

2 garlic cloves, crushed

1½ teaspoons ground cumin

1½ teaspoons ancho chilli powder

½ teaspoon sea salt

½ teaspoon freshly cracked black pepper

TO SERVE

12 warm Flour tortillas (page 12)

Guacamole (page 34)

Mexican crema, sour cream or crème fraîche

Red tomato salsa (page 29)

Place all the marinade ingredients in a bowl and whisk to combine. Add the chicken breasts, capsicum and onion, tossing to coat in the marinade. Cover and refrigerate for 30 minutes.

Heat a chargrill pan over high heat and cook the chicken breasts for about 5—7 minutes on each side, or until cooked through. Remove, keep warm and set aside to rest.

Grill the capsicum and onion, turning often, for 10—12 minutes, until tender and slightly charred.

Slice the chicken into strips. To serve, place some chicken on a warm tortilla. Add some grilled vegetables, then top with guacamole, crema and tomato salsa. Serve immediately.

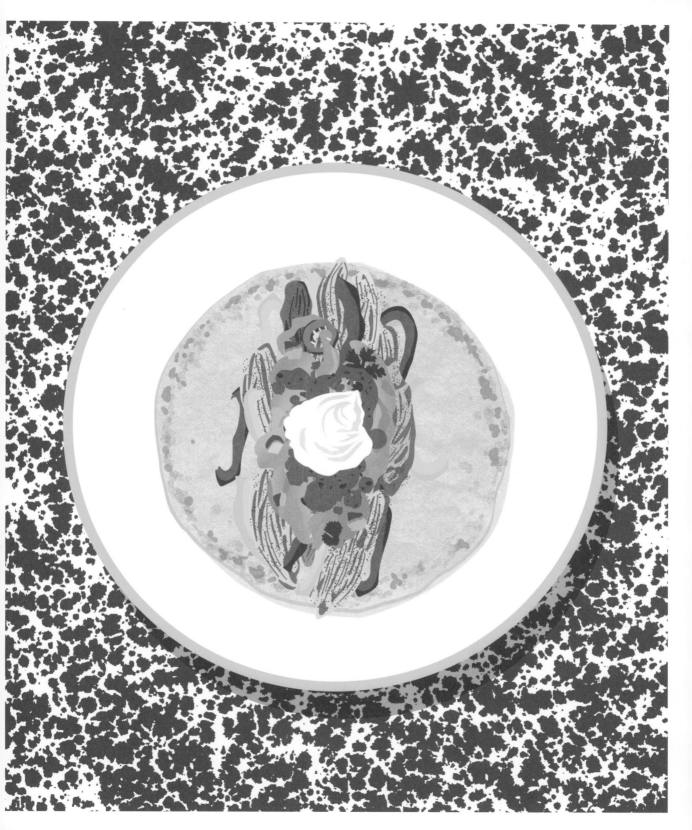

BBQ SPICE-RUBBED CHICKEN TACOS

MAKES 12 TACOS / SERVES 4

2½ tablespoons olive oil

3 boneless chicken breasts, about 750 g (1 lb 11 oz), skin removed

6 whole spring onions (scallions), roots trimmed

BBQ SPICE RUB

1 tablespoon panela (see Note) or brown sugar

2 teaspoons ground cumin

2 teaspoons ancho chilli powder

2 teaspoons smoked paprika

1½ teaspoons ground coriander

1 teaspoon cayenne pepper

1 teaspoon ground cinnamon

1 teaspoon garlic powder

1 teaspoon onion powder

1 teaspoon fine sea salt

½ teaspoon freshly cracked black pepper

TO SERVE

12 warm Corn tortillas (page 15)

sliced pickled jalapeño chillies

Red chilli sauce (page 32)

Roasted tomato salsa (page 30)

12 lime wedges

chopped coriander (cilantro)

Place the spice rub ingredients in a bowl and stir to combine.

Stir through 2 tablespoons of the oil, then add the chicken breasts, tossing to thoroughly them coat in all the spices. Set aside for 15 minutes to marinate.

Heat a chargrill pan over high heat and cook the chicken breasts for about 5 — 7 minutes on each side, or until cooked through. Remove, keep warm and rest for 3 — 4 minutes before slicing.

In the same pan, add the remaining oil and grill the spring onions for 2 — 3 minutes, or until lightly charred and cooked. Slice into quarters.

To serve, place some chicken on a warm tortilla. Top with two spring onion quarters, pickled jalapeño, chilli sauce and salsa. Squeeze over some lime, sprinkle with coriander and serve immediately.

NOTE

Panela is an unrefined cane sugar, typically used in Latin American recipes.

PORK TACOS

CARNITAS STREET TACOS

MAKES 12 TACOS / SERVES 6

500 g (1 lb 2 oz) lard

1 kg (2 lb 3 oz) pork shoulder, cut into 5 — 6 cm (2 — 2½ inch) dice

1½ tablespoons panela (see Note) or brown sugar

3 teaspoons flaked sea salt

3 teaspoons ancho chilli powder

4 garlic cloves, peeled and smashed

1 small brown onion, peeled and quartered

1 orange, skin left on, cut into quarters

1 bay leaf

1 cinnamon stick

TO SERVE

12 warm Corn tortillas (page 15)

1 small brown onion, diced

Fresh tomatillo salsa verde (page 24)

½ cup chopped coriander (cilantro) leaves

12 lime wedges

Preheat the oven to 145°C (285°F).

Melt the lard in a large flameproof casserole dish over medium heat. While it is melting, toss the pork cubes in a large bowl with the panela, salt and chilli powder, coating completely and evenly. Place the seasoned pork into the melted lard with the remaining ingredients, then increase the heat and bring just to the boil.

Remove from the heat, put the lid on and transfer the dish to the oven. Cook for 2½ — 3 hours, or until the pork is cooked through and is fork-tender.

Remove the pork from the lard mixture. When cool enough to handle, shred the meat into pieces, using two forks to pull it apart.

Serve immediately on warm tortillas, topped with onion, salsa verde, coriander and a squeeze of lime.

If not serving immediately, save some of the lard to use when reheating the pork: place a tablespoon of lard in a frying pan over high heat, add some shredded pork, and fry until crispy and browned.

NOTE

Panela is an unrefined cane sugar, typically used in Latin American recipes.

CHILORIO TACOS

MAKES 12 TACOS / SERVES 6

1.5 kg (3 lb 5 oz) boneless pork shoulder, cut into 4 pieces

2 bay leaves

10 black peppercorns

2 tablespoons lard or olive oil

CHILORIO ADOBO SAUCE

2 dried guajillo chillies, stems and seeds removed

4 dried ancho chillies, stems and seeds removed

6 garlic cloves, peeled

2 teaspoons ground cumin

2 teaspoons dried Mexican oregano (see Note)

$\frac{1}{4}$ teaspoon ground allspice

125 ml (4 fl oz/$\frac{1}{2}$ cup) white vinegar

80 ml (2$\frac{1}{2}$ fl oz/$\frac{1}{3}$ cup) orange juice

zest of 1 large orange

1 teaspoon ground black pepper

1$\frac{1}{2}$ teaspoons sea salt

TO SERVE

12 warm Corn tortillas (page 15), about 15 cm (6 inches) in size

Red pickled onion (page 36), or diced white onion

crumbled queso fresco or mild feta cheese

chopped coriander (cilantro) leaves

Chipotle crema (page 104)

12 lime wedges

Place the pork in a large saucepan over medium — high heat. Cover with water and add the bay leaves and peppercorns. Bring to the boil, then reduce the heat to low, cover and simmer for 2$\frac{1}{2}$ — 3 hours, or until the pork is fork-tender and easily shredded. Allow to cool, then shred the meat using two forks.

To make the chilorio adobo sauce, place the chillies in a bowl, cover with boiling water and set aside for 20 minutes to rehydrate. When softened, add 185 ml (6 fl oz/$\frac{3}{4}$ cup) of the chilli soaking water to a blender. Add the softened chillies and all the remaining sauce ingredients. Process until a smooth paste is formed.

Add the lard or oil to a large saucepan over medium heat and warm through. Carefully add the chilorio adobo sauce, as it may splatter, and cook for about 7 — 10 minutes. Add the shredded pork and stir it through, coating the meat in the sauce. Taste and adjust the seasoning, adding more salt if desired. Cook for a further 10 — 15 minutes, or until the meat has absorbed all of the sauce.

To serve, place some meat on a warm tortilla, then top with onion, crumbled cheese, coriander and a drizzle of chipotle crema. Finish with a squeeze of lime and serve immediately.

NOTE

Mexican oregano is related to lemon verbena, and has grassy, lime citrus notes. It can be bought online or from specialty Latin grocery stores.

CHORIZO, POTATO & FRIED EGG TACOS

MAKES 8 TACOS / SERVES 4

1 large potato, scrubbed but not peeled, cut into 2 cm (¾ inch) dice

3 tablespoons olive oil

½ teaspoon smoked paprika

400 g (14 oz) Mexican chorizo sausages, removed from their casings

1 small onion, diced

2 tablespoons butter

8 small eggs

1 teaspoon chilli flakes

TO SERVE

Refried beans (page 17)

8 warm Corn tortillas (page 15)

shredded cheese of your choice

Roasted tomato salsa (page 30) or Roasted tomatillo salsa verde (page 24)

Mexican crema, sour cream or crème fraîche

Red chilli sauce (page 32)

coriander (cilantro) leaves

Mexican red rice (page 19)

Place the potato cubes in a small saucepan of water and bring to the boil over high heat. Reduce the heat to a high simmer, then cook for 4 minutes, or until soft and cooked through. Drain and set aside.

Heat 1 tablespoon of the oil in a frying pan over medium — high heat. Add the potato and paprika, season with sea salt and freshly cracked black pepper, and cook for 5 — 6 minutes, stirring often, until golden brown and crispy. Remove from the pan and keep warm.

In the same pan, sauté the chorizo and onion over medium — high heat for 5 — 7 minutes, until the chorizo is cooked through and the onion is soft and translucent. Combine with the potato, and keep warm while frying the eggs.

In a large frying pan, large enough to hold all the eggs, place the remaining 2 tablespoons oil and butter over medium heat. When the oil is warm and the butter has melted, crack the eggs into the pan. Increase the heat to get the egg whites sizzling, then cook for 2 — 3 minutes, until all the whites are just cooked through and firm. Season with salt, pepper and the chilli flakes.

To serve, place a spoonful of refried beans on a warm tortilla, then top with some chorizo mixture and cheese. Add some salsa, a dollop of crema and chilli sauce, and a sprinkling of coriander to finish. Serve immediately, with Mexican red rice on the side.

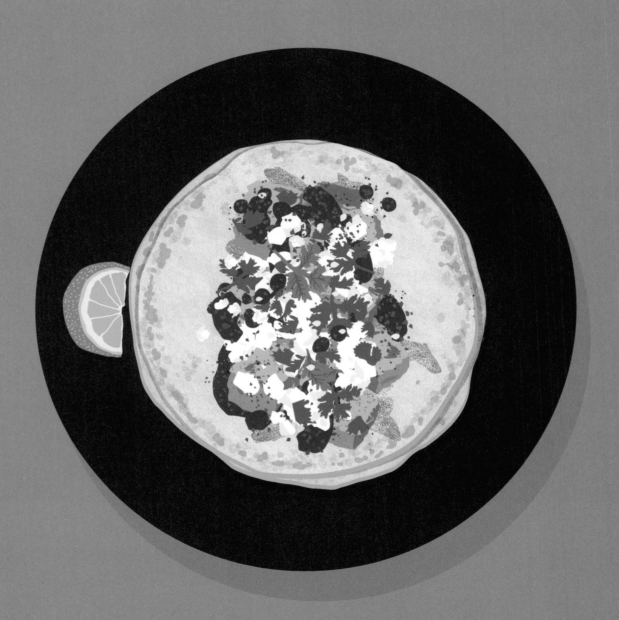

PORK CHILLI VERDE TACOS

MAKES 12 TACOS / SERVES 4

60 ml (2 fl oz/¼ cup) olive oil

1 kg (2 lb 3 oz) pork shoulder,
cut into 4 cm (1½ inch) dice

1 teaspoon sea salt

1 teaspoon freshly cracked black pepper

1½ teaspoons ground cumin

1½ teaspoons ground coriander

1 bay leaf

½ cup chopped coriander (cilantro)
leaves

VERDE SAUCE

1 large brown onion, quartered

4 fresh poblano chillies, halved, stems
and seeds removed

4 fresh green jalapeño chillies, halved,
stems and half of the seeds removed

500 g (1 lb 2 oz) tomatillos, husks
removed, rinsed

4 large garlic cloves, peeled

1½ teaspoons dried Mexican
oregano (see Notes)

500 ml (17 fl oz/2 cups) chicken
stock

TO SERVE

24 warm Corn tortillas (see Note;
page 15)

crumbled queso fresco or mild feta
cheese

coriander (cilantro) leaves

lime wedges

Mexican red rice (page 19)

Black beans in the pot (page 16)

Heat an oven grill (broiler) to medium — high. To make the verde sauce, place the onion, chillies, tomatillos and garlic cloves on a baking tray and grill (broil) for 10 — 15 minutes, turning once, until softened and lightly charred. Remove and set aside, placing the chillies in a bowl and covering with plastic wrap to steam for 10 minutes. Peel and discard the skin from the chillies. Place the chillies in a blender with the onion, tomatillos and garlic, add the remaining sauce ingredients and blitz until puréed. Set aside.

Heat the oil in a large flameproof casserole dish over medium — high heat. Sear the pork in batches for 4 — 5 minutes, or until well browned, removing each batch to a plate.

Return all the pork to the pan. Add the salt, pepper, ground spices and bay leaf and pour in most of the verde sauce, stirring well. Bring the mixture to the boil, then cover, reduce the heat to low and simmer for 2½ — 3 hours, or until the pork is tender and the sauce has reduced.

Just before serving, stir the coriander leaves through the pork mixture.

To serve, stack two warm tortillas on top of each other, to make a double layer. Top with some pork, cheese, more coriander and a squeeze of lime. Serve immediately, with red rice and beans, spooning the remaining verde sauce over the rice.

NOTES

Tacos with a wet stew-like filling ('guisado'), such as these, often use two tortillas instead of a single tortilla as a base.
Mexican oregano is related to lemon verbena, and has grassy, lime citrus notes. It can be bought online or from specialty Latin grocery stores.

SWEET BAHN MI PORK BELLY TACOS

MAKES 12 TACOS / SERVES 6

2 tablespoons sea salt

1 teaspoon freshly cracked black pepper

1 teaspoon ground white pepper

1.2 kg (2 lb 10 oz) pork belly, skin on and scored (ask your butcher to do this), refrigerated overnight without being covered

QUICK PICKLE CABBAGE SLAW

125 ml (4 fl oz/½ cup) white vinegar

110 g (4 oz/½ cup) white sugar

1 teaspoon sea salt

75 g (2¾ oz/1 cup) shredded white cabbage

1 small carrot, julienned

1 small Lebanese (short) cucumber, julienned

½ small red onion, thinly sliced

1 red bird's eye chilli, thinly sliced

SWEET GLAZE

2 tablespoons kecap manis

2 tablespoons honey

1 tablespoon brown sugar

60 ml (2 fl oz/¼ cup) soy sauce

2 tablespoons chopped coriander

TO SERVE

125 g (4½ oz) chicken liver pâté

12 warm Flour tortillas (page 12)

kewpie mayonnaise

coriander (cilantro) leaves

1 red bird's eye chilli, thinly sliced

Preheat the oven to 220°C (430°F).

Mix together the salt and black and white pepper, then rub all over the pork. Place the pork on a wire rack set over a baking tray, then roast in the oven for 30 minutes.

Reduce the oven temperature to 170°C (340°F) and roast for a further 1 — 1½ hours, or until the pork is tender and cooked through, and the skin is crisp. Remove from the oven and rest for 20 — 25 minutes.

Meanwhile, to make the slaw, combine the vinegar, sugar and salt in a saucepan over low heat and stir to dissolve. Allow to cool, then pour over the remaining slaw ingredients and mix well to combine. Cover and refrigerate for 30 minutes before using; the slaw will keep for 2 days in a clean airtight container in the fridge.

Slice the rested pork into 36 equal pieces. Mix together the sweet glaze ingredients, then brush all over the flesh of the pork.

Place a frying pan over medium — high heat and sear the glazed meat for about 10 — 15 seconds on each side, until sticky and caramelised.

To serve, spread some pâté on a warm tortilla, then top with some slaw and glazed pork. Drizzle with mayonnaise, top with coriander and chilli and serve immediately.

YUCATÁN 'COCHINITA PIBIL' TACOS

MAKES 12 TACOS / SERVES 6

1.5 kg (3 lb 5 oz) boneless pork shoulder, cut into 6 pieces
3 teaspoons sea salt
banana leaves (see Notes), for lining
1 large onion, sliced

ACHIOTE MARINADE

10 roasted garlic cloves, peeled
½ cinnamon stick, roasted and ground
2 cloves, roasted and ground
1½ teaspoons cumin seeds, roasted
75 g (2¾ oz) achiote paste (see Notes)
1 teaspoon each ancho chilli powder, dried Mexican oregano and pepper
125 ml (4 fl oz/½ cup) orange juice
60 ml (2 fl oz/¼ cup) lime juice

ROASTED TOMATO COOKING SAUCE

400 g (14 oz) tomatoes, roasted
4 roasted garlic cloves, peeled
1 roasted fresh red jalapeño chilli, seeds left in, stem removed
¼ cup chopped coriander (cilantro)
80 ml (2½ fl oz/⅓ cup) orange juice
30 ml (1½ tablespoons) lime juice
1 teaspoon each sea salt and pepper

TO SERVE

12 warm Corn tortillas (page 15)
Red pickled onion (page 36)
sliced fresh habanero chillies
coriander (cilantro) leaves
Habanero hot sauce (page 28)
12 lime wedges

Rub the pork all over with the salt, then place in a large bowl and set aside.

Place all the achiote marinade ingredients in a blender and blitz to combine. Pour the marinade over the pork, turning to coat completely. Cover and marinate in the fridge for 4 hours, or preferably overnight.

Preheat the oven to 150°C (300°F). Place all the ingredients for the roasted tomato cooking sauce in a blender and blitz to a purée.

Line a large flameproof casserole dish with banana leaves. Add the pork, then cover with the cooking sauce, and scatter the onion slices over. Fold the banana leaves over, covering the pork completely. Cover with a tight-fitting lid, transfer to the oven and cook for 3 — 3½ hours, or until the meat is very tender.

Remove from the oven and leave until cool enough to handle. Remove and discard the banana leaves, then shred the meat using two forks to pull it apart. Return the pork to the pan and warm it through in the cooking sauce.

To serve, place some pork on a warm tortilla, then top with pickled onion, habanero chilli slices, coriander and a splash of hot sauce. Add a squeeze of lime and serve immediately.

NOTES

Banana leaves are available from Asian grocery stores.
Achiote paste is a Yucatán condiment made with bright red annatto seeds, tomatoes and spices. You'll find it in Latin grocery stores and online.

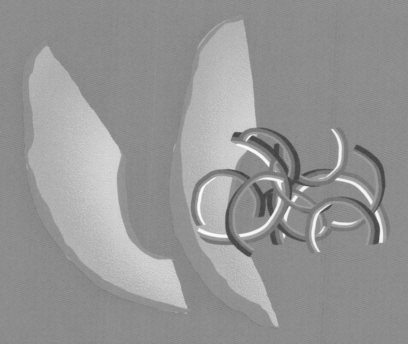

BEEF TACOS

GRILLED CARNE ASADA TACOS

MAKES 12 TACOS / SERVES 4

1 kg (2 lb 3 oz) skirt steak

LIME, LEMON & CHIPOTLE MARINADE

80 ml (2½ fl oz/⅓ cup) olive oil

1 large onion, thinly sliced

4 garlic cloves, crushed

60 ml (2 fl oz/¼ cup) lime juice

60 ml (2 fl oz/¼ cup) lemon juice

3 teaspoons ground cumin

3 teaspoons chipotle chilli powder

2½ teaspoons freshly cracked black pepper

1 teaspoon sea salt

TO SERVE

12 warm Corn tortillas (page 15)

Pico de gallo (page 34)

2 avocados, sliced

sliced pickled jalapeño chillies

chopped coriander (cilantro)

12 lime wedges

Place all the marinade ingredients in a large bowl and whisk together. Add the steak, toss to coat, then cover and refrigerate for 3 — 4 hours, or overnight.

When ready to serve, grill the steak over medium heat for 6 — 7 minutes, turning once. Allow to rest for 4 — 5 minutes, then slice into strips.

To serve, place some steak on a warm tortilla. Top with pico de gallo, avocado slices, pickled jalapeño, coriander and a squeeze of lime. Serve immediately.

CUBAN BEEF PICADILLO TACOS

MAKES 12 TACOS / SERVES 6

60 ml (2 fl oz/¼ cup) olive oil

500 g (1 lb 2 oz) minced (ground) beef

1 potato, peeled and cut into 1 cm (½ inch) dice

1 carrot, cut into 1 cm (½ inch) dice

1 brown onion, thinly sliced

4 garlic cloves, crushed

3 teaspoons ground cumin

2 teaspoons smoked paprika

2 teaspoons mild chilli powder

1 teaspoon freshly cracked black pepper

375 ml (12½ fl oz/1½ cups) tomato passata (puréed tomatoes)

80 ml (2½ fl oz/⅓ cup) white vinegar

85 g (3 oz/½ cup) pimento-stuffed whole green olives

40 g (1½ oz/⅓ cup) sultanas (golden raisins)

3 tablespoons baby capers, drained

1 teaspoon sea salt, or to taste

TO SERVE

shredded iceberg lettuce

12 warm Flour tortillas (page 12), about 15 cm (6 inches) in size

mixed shredded cheese, such as oaxaca, mozzarella and cheddar

thinly sliced avocado

Mexican crema, sour cream or crème fraîche

Pickled taqueria-style vegetables (page 37)

Place a large frying pan over medium heat and add the oil. Add the beef and cook for about 5 minutes, or until lightly browned, breaking up any lumps. Stir in the potato and carrot and cook for 3 — 4 minutes, then add the onion and cook for a further 4 minutes. Stir in the garlic and spices, sautéing for 1 — 2 minutes before adding in the remaining ingredients. Cook at a medium to low simmer for 20 minutes, stirring occasionally.

To serve, place some shredded lettuce on a warm tortilla, top with some of the beef mixture, then some cheese, avocado slices and crema. Serve immediately, with pickled vegetables on the side.

SHREDDED BRISKET TACOS

MAKES 24 TACOS / SERVES 8

1.5 kg (3 lb 5 oz) beef brisket, cut into 8 even pieces

60 ml (2 fl oz/¼ cup) olive oil

1 large carrot, roughly diced

1 large onion, roughly diced

4 — 5 large garlic cloves, roughly chopped

1 tablespoon ground ancho chilli powder

2 teaspoons ground cumin

500 ml (17 fl oz/2 cups) tomato passata (puréed tomatoes)

750 ml (25½ fl oz/3 cups) beef stock

2 teaspoons apple cider vinegar

1 bay leaf

1 tablespoon dried Mexican oregano (see Note)

TO SERVE

24 warm Flour tortillas (page 12), about 15 cm (6 inches) in size

Pico de gallo (page 34)

avocado slices

Mexican crema, sour cream or crème fraîche

chopped coriander (cilantro) leaves

Green chilli sauce (page 33)

Preheat the oven to 160°C (320°F).

Season the beef well with sea salt and freshly cracked black pepper. Heat the oil in a large flameproof casserole dish over medium — high heat. Add the meat in batches, searing on all sides for about 4 — 5 minutes, or until well browned. Set the meat aside.

Turn the heat down slightly, add the carrot and onion, stirring, and cook for 5 — 6 minutes. Add the garlic, chilli powder and cumin, and cook for another 1 — 2 minutes, stirring constantly. Add the remaining ingredients, including the beef, then increase the heat and bring just to the boil.

Cover with a tight-fitting lid, then transfer to the oven. Cook for 2½ — 3 hours, or until the beef is fork-tender. Set the meat aside, allow to cool slightly, then shred into pieces using two forks to pull the meat apart.

Place the casserole dish containing the sauce back on the stovetop over high heat. Leave to cook for 6 — 7 minutes to reduce the sauce slightly, until you have about 375 — 500 ml (12½ — 17 fl oz/1½ — 2 cups) of sauce. Purée the sauce, then add the shredded meat and stir through to combine.

To serve, place some of the brisket on a warm tortilla. Add some pico de gallo, avocado slices, crema, coriander and a dash of green chilli sauce. Serve immediately.

NOTE

Mexican oregano is related to lemon verbena, and has grassy, lime citrus notes. It can be bought online or from specialty Latin grocery stores.

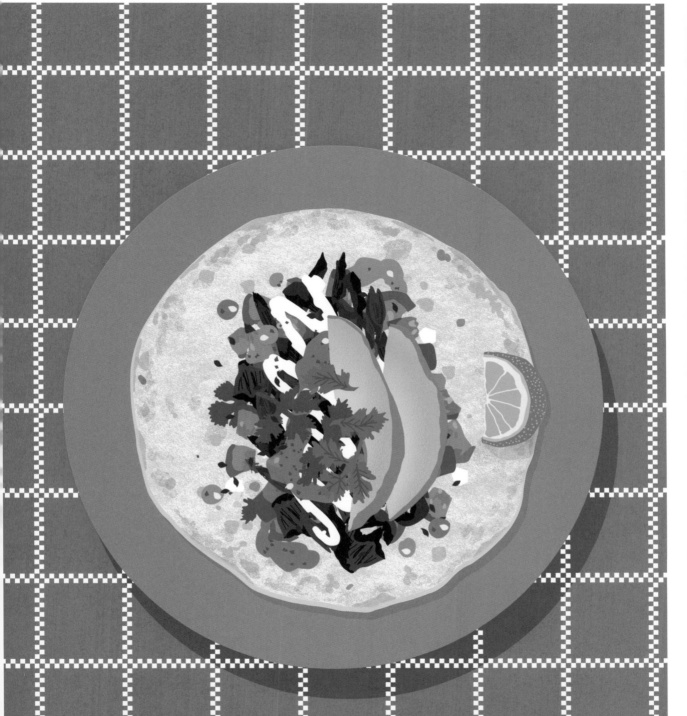

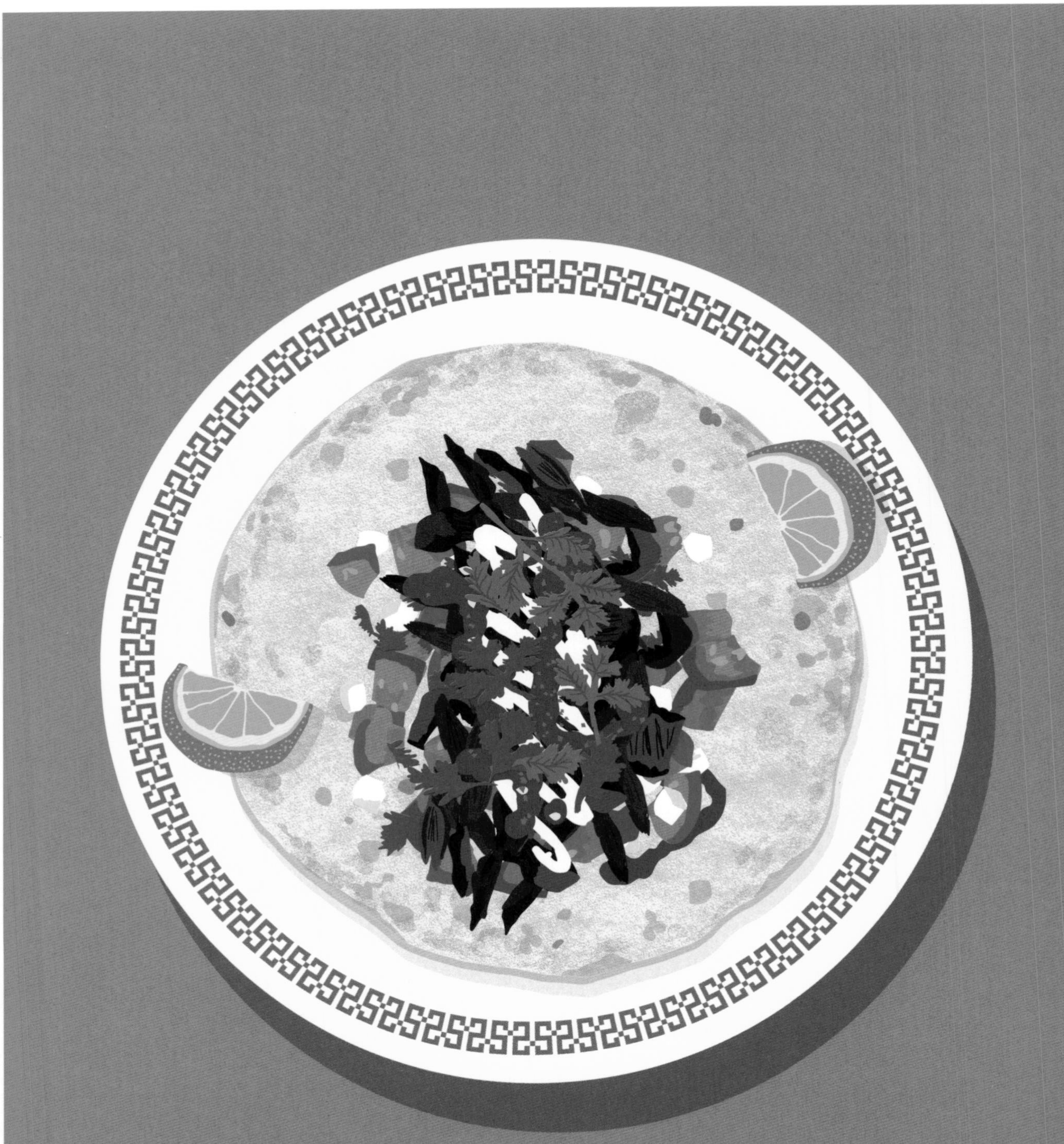

BEEF CHEEK TACOS

MAKES 12 TACOS / SERVES 6

1 kg (2 lb 3 oz) beef cheeks

½ teaspoon sea salt

½ teaspoon freshly cracked black pepper

2 tablespoons olive oil

1 large brown onion, diced

1 bay leaf

½ cinnamon stick

750 ml (25½ fl oz/3 cups) beef stock

3 teaspoons red wine vinegar

CHILLI COOKING SAUCE

4 guajillo chillies, seeds and stems removed

3 morita chillies, seeds and stems removed

6 garlic cloves, peeled

2 teaspoons dried Mexican oregano (see Note)

2 teaspoons ground cumin

2 teaspoons ground coriander

¼ teaspoon ground cloves

TO SERVE

12 warm Corn tortillas (page 15)

Pico de gallo (page 34)

Red chilli sauce (page 32)

Mexican crema, sour cream or crème fraîche

coriander (cilantro) leaves

Mexican red rice (page 19)

Black refried beans (page 17)

To make the chilli cooking sauce, place a cast-iron pan or chargrill pan over medium — high heat and dry-roast the chillies for 15 — 30 seconds, turning them so they don't burn. Remove and place in a bowl, cover with boiling water and leave to rehydrate for 20 minutes. Drain, reserving 250 ml (8½ fl oz/1 cup) of the chilli soaking liquid for the sauce, then purée together with the remaining cooking sauce ingredients and set aside.

Season the beef cheeks with the salt and pepper. Place a large flameproof casserole dish over medium — high heat, add the oil, and then sear the beef for 5 — 6 minutes, or until browned all over. Remove from the casserole dish and set aside.

Sauté the onion in the casserole dish for 5 — 7 minutes, or until golden, then add the cooking sauce, bay leaf, cinnamon stick, stock and all the beef. Bring to the boil, then cover and reduce to a low simmer. Cook for about 2½ — 3 hours, or until the meat is tender and easily shreds with a fork. Remove from the heat.

When cool enough to handle, shred the meat using two forks to pull it apart. Toss the shredded beef through the sauce, stir in the vinegar, and season with more salt and pepper to taste.

To serve, place some shredded beef on a warm tortilla, then top with pico de gallo, red chilli sauce, crema and coriander. Serve immediately, with red rice and refried beans on the side.

NOTE

Mexican oregano is related to lemon verbena, and has grassy, lime citrus notes. It can be bought online or from specialty Latin grocery stores.

BEEF SHORT RIBS

MAKES 18 TACOS / SERVES 6

4 dried pasilla chillies, seeds and stems removed

2 dried cascabel chillies, seeds and stems removed

4 chipotle chillies in adobo sauce

4 large beef short ribs on the bone, about 1.5 kg (3 lb 5 oz) in total

1 teaspoon sea salt

1 teaspoon freshly cracked black pepper

60 ml (2 fl oz/¼ cup) olive oil

1 large brown onion, sliced

4 garlic cloves, crushed

2 teaspoons ground cumin

2 teaspoons dried Mexican oregano (see Note)

440 ml (15 fl oz) dark Mexican beer

750 ml (25½ fl oz/3 cups) chicken stock, approximately

CHIPOTLE CREMA

250 g (9 oz/1 cup) Mexican crema, sour cream or crème fraîche

2 chipotle chillies in adobo sauce, plus 2 teaspoons of the sauce

1 tablespoon lime juice

TO SERVE

18 warm Corn tortillas (page 15)

crumbled queso fresco or mild feta cheese

chopped white onion

coriander (cilantro) leaves

18 lime wedges

Place a cast-iron pan or chargrill pan over medium — high heat and dry-roast the dried chillies for 15 — 30 seconds, turning them so they don't burn. Remove and place in a bowl, cover with boiling water and leave to rehydrate for 20 minutes. Drain and place in a blender with the chipotle chillies and blitz to a purée. Set aside.

Season the beef ribs with the salt and pepper. Place a large flameproof casserole dish over medium — high heat, add the oil, then sear the ribs on all sides for 5 — 6 minutes, or until browned. Remove from the casserole dish and set aside.

Sauté the onion in the casserole dish for 6 — 7 minutes, or until a light golden brown. Add the garlic, cumin and oregano and cook for a further minute. Return the ribs to the pan, add the puréed chillies, then pour in the beer and 500 ml (17 fl oz/2 cups) of the chicken stock. Bring to the boil. Cover with a tight-fitting lid and reduce the heat to a low simmer and cook for 2 hours.

Check the liquid level and add the remaining 250 ml (8½ fl oz/1 cup) stock if needed. Simmer for a further 1 — 1½ hours, or until the meat is cooked through, very tender and falling off the bone. Remove from the heat.

To make the chipotle crema, blitz all the ingredients together in a blender and refrigerate until required; it will keep for 4 — 5 days in a clean airtight container in the fridge.

When cool enough to handle, shred the meat using two forks to pull it apart, then stir it back through the cooking sauce. Season with more salt and pepper to taste.

To serve, place some beef mixture on a warm tortilla, then sprinkle with cheese, onion and coriander. Finish with a drizzle of chipotle crema and a squeeze of lime and serve immediately.

NOTE

Mexican oregano is related to lemon verbena, and has grassy, lime citrus notes. It can be bought online or from specialty Latin grocery stores.

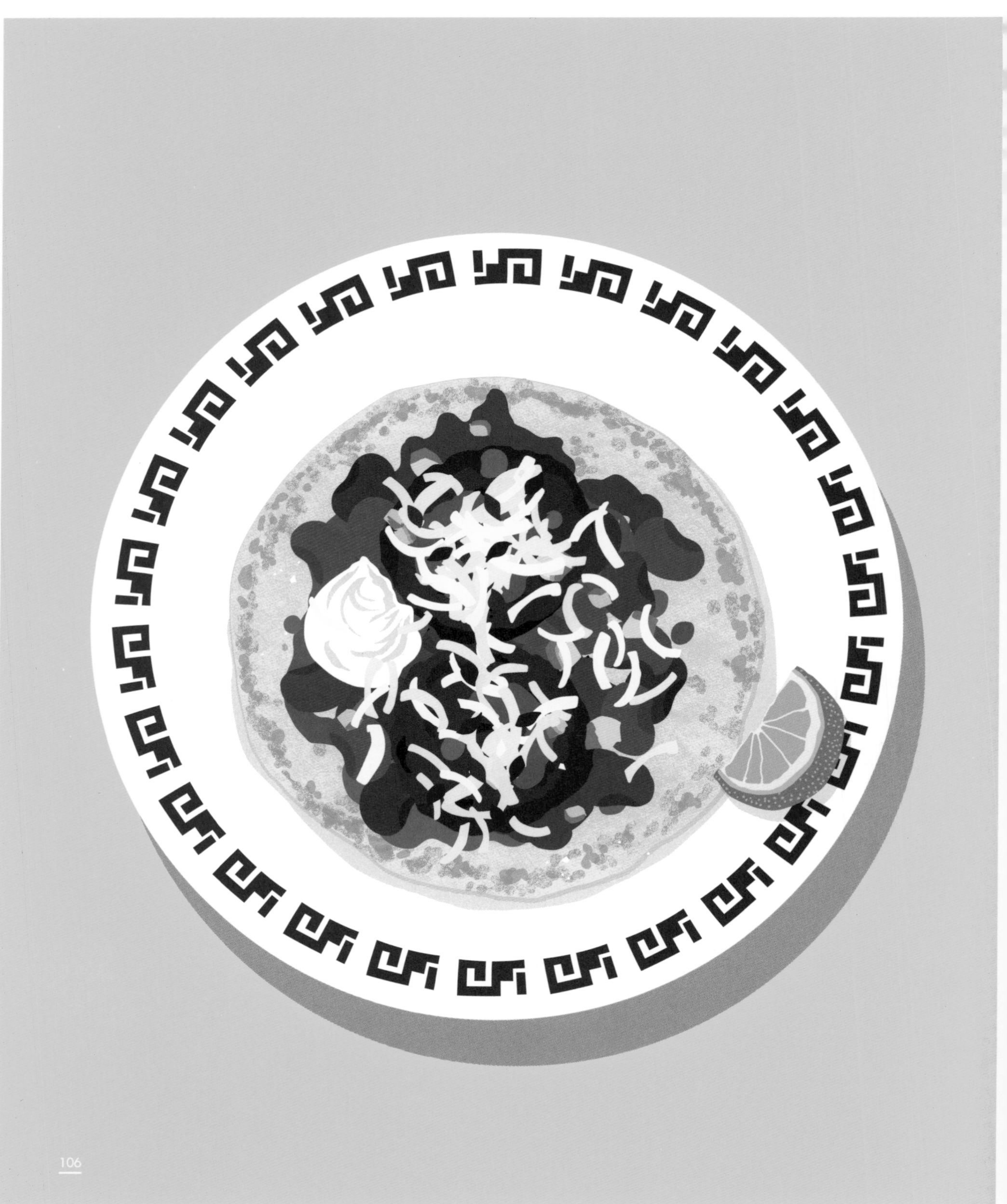

MEATBALL TACOS IN CHIPOTLE ADOBO

MAKES 8 TACOS / SERVES 4

MEATBALLS

100 g (3½ oz) Mexican chorizo

400 g (14 oz) minced (ground) beef

90 g (3 oz/½ cup) cooked medium-grain rice

1 egg

1 small brown onion, finely chopped

¼ cup chopped coriander (cilantro)

1 teaspoon dried Mexican oregano (see Notes) or regular oregano

1 teaspoon each dried epazote (see Notes) and ground cumin

½ teaspoon each salt and pepper

CHIPOTLE ADOBO SAUCE

80 ml (2½ fl oz/⅓ cup) olive oil

1 brown onion, diced

2 garlic cloves, finely crushed

2 x 400 g (14 oz) tins chopped tomatoes

6 chipotle chillies in adobo sauce, diced, plus 2 tablespoons of the sauce

2 teaspoons white vinegar

1 teaspoon dried Mexican oregano

TO SERVE

Mexican red rice (page 19),
Pinto beans in the pot (page 16)

8 warm Flour tortillas (page 12), about 15 cm (6 inches) in size

crumbled oaxaca and cotija cheese

chopped oregano and coriander (cilantro)

Mexican crema or sour cream

8 lime wedges

Remove and discard the casing from the chorizo sausage and place the sausage and all the remaining meatball ingredients in a large bowl and mix together well. Divide the mixture into 16 equal portions and roll into balls. Place on a tray, cover and refrigerate while making the chipotle adobo sauce.

To make the sauce, place a large wide saucepan over medium — low heat, add the oil and gently cook the onion for about 8 — 9 minutes, or until soft and translucent. Add the garlic and cook for another minute, then stir in the remaining sauce ingredients and simmer over low heat for 25 minutes. Taste the sauce and season with salt and pepper.

Add the meatballs to the pan. Increase the heat, just bringing the sauce up to the boil, then simmer over low heat for 25 — 30 minutes, until the meatballs are cooked through and the sauce has reduced slightly.

To serve, place some rice and beans on a warm tortilla. Top with a spoonful of sauce, then two meatballs and a bit more sauce. Sprinkle with the cheeses and herbs, add a dollop of crema and a squeeze of lime and serve immediately.

NOTES

If you like, replace the oaxaca and cotija cheeses with mild feta and mozzarella.

Mexican oregano is related to lemon verbena, and has grassy, lime citrus notes. It can be bought online or from specialty Latin grocery stores.

Epazote is a herb used in Mexican cuisine. It can be purchased from specialty grocery stores or online.

DRINKS

PINEAPPLE AGUA FRESCA

MAKES ABOUT 2.6 LITRES (88 FL OZ) / SERVES 8

1 kg (2 lb 3 oz) pineapple flesh, puréed and strained, to yield about 750 ml (25½ fl oz/3 cups)

60 — 80 ml (2 — 2½ fl oz/¼ — ⅓ cup) lime juice, to taste

1 lime, sliced into thin half-moons

6 lemon verbena sprigs, plus extra to garnish each glass

ice cubes

SUGAR SYRUP

115 g (4 oz/½ cup) caster (superfine) sugar

125 ml (4 fl oz/½ cup) water

To make the sugar syrup, place the sugar and water in a small saucepan over high heat and bring to the boil. Reduce the heat to a rapid simmer and cook for 1 — 2 minutes, or until the sugar has dissolved. Cool before using; the syrup will keep for up to 2 weeks in a clean airtight container in the fridge, and makes about 125 ml (4 fl oz/½ cup).

Pour the pineapple juice, lime juice and sugar syrup into a large container. Add the lime slices, herb sprigs and 1.8 litres (61 fl oz) water. Stir well and taste, adding more lime juice or sugar syrup if desired. Refrigerate until chilled.

To serve, pour into ice-filled glasses and garnish with extra herbs.

NOTES

Instead of sugar syrup, use honey or agave syrup if desired.
Besides lemon verbena, other fresh herbs that pair well with pineapple include mint, lemon balm and lemon thyme.

WATERMELON & BASIL AGUA FRESCA

MAKES ABOUT 2.6 LITRES (88 FL OZ) / SERVES 8

1.5 kg (3 lb 5 oz) seedless watermelon flesh, puréed and strained, to yield about 1.4 litres (47 fl oz)

80 ml (2½ fl oz/⅓ cup) lime juice

125 ml (4 fl oz/½ cup) Sugar syrup (page 110)

1 lime, sliced into half moons

6 purple basil sprigs, plus extra to garnish each glass

ice cubes

Pour the watermelon juice, lime juice and sugar syrup into a large container. Add the lime slices, herb sprigs and 1 litre (34 fl oz/4 cups) water. Stir well and taste, adding more lime juice or sugar syrup if desired. Refrigerate until chilled.

To serve, pour into ice-filled glasses and garnish with extra herbs.

NOTES

Use honey or agave syrup instead of sugar syrup, if desired.
Other fresh herbs that are great with watermelon include Italian basil, mint and lemon balm.

MICHELADA

MAKES 1

2 teaspoons smoked sea salt flakes

1 lime wedge

ice cubes

1 tablespoon lime juice

2 — 3 dashes hot sauce

355 ml (12 fl oz) bottle of Mexican lager

Place the salt on a small plate. Run the lime wedge around the rim of a beer glass, then dip the rim in the salt to coat.

Add ice to the glass, along with the lime juice and hot sauce. Pour in the beer, garnish with the lime wedge and serve.

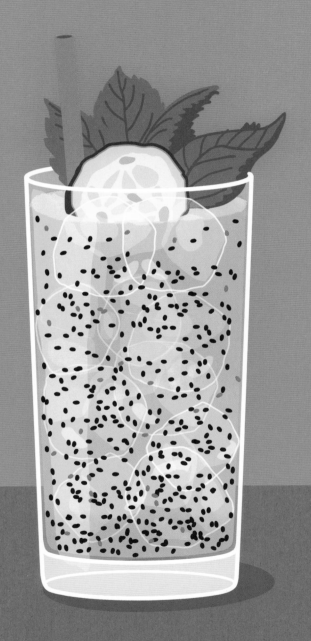

LIME, CUCUMBER & CHIA AGUA FRESCA

MAKES ABOUT 1.5 LITRES (51 FL OZ) / SERVES 4—6

1 telegraph (long) cucumber, roughly chopped and puréed

90 ml (3 fl oz) lime juice

90 ml (3 fl oz) Sugar syrup (page 110)

1 tablespoon chia seeds

3 mint sprigs

ice cubes

extra mint, lime or cucumber slices, to garnish

Pour the cucumber juice, lime juice and sugar syrup into a large container. Add the chia seeds, herb sprigs and 1 litre (34 fl oz/ 4 cups) water. Stir well and taste, adding more lime juice or sugar syrup if desired. Refrigerate until chilled.

To serve, pour into ice-filled glasses and garnish with extra cucumber, lime slices or herbs.

NOTE

Instead of sugar syrup, use honey or agave syrup if desired.

PISTACHIO HORCHATA

MAKES ABOUT 1 LITRE (34 FL OZ) / SERVES 4

250 g (9 oz/1¼ cups) uncooked jasmine rice

75 g (2½ oz/½ cup) pistachio nuts, plus extra chopped nuts to garnish

1 cinnamon stick, broken into pieces

6 cardamom pods, cracked

1 plump vanilla bean, split in half lengthways, or 2 teaspoons vanilla paste

175 g (6 oz/½ cup) raw honey, or to taste

ice cubes

ground cinnamon, to garnish

Place the rice, pistachio nuts, cinnamon stick and cardamom pods in a large bowl. If using a vanilla bean, add it now as well. Pour in 750 ml (25½ fl oz/3 cups) boiling water, then cover and set aside to soak for 6 — 8 hours.

Place the ingredients in a blender and process on high until smooth. Strain into a jug through a sieve lined with muslin (cheesecloth), discarding the solids.

Add the honey, 250 ml (8½ fl oz/1 cup) cold water and the vanilla paste, if using. Blend the liquid again, then strain a final time. Taste and adjust the sweetness if desired.

To serve, pour into ice-filled glasses, then garnish with extra chopped pistachio nuts and a sprinkling of ground cinnamon.

COCO-LOCO

MAKES 1

125 ml (4 fl oz/½ cup) coconut milk

100 ml (3½ fl oz) coconut water

45 ml (1½ fl oz) spiced rum

40 ml (1¼ fl oz) lime juice

100 g (3½ oz) frozen pineapple pieces

1 teaspoon panela (see Note) or agave syrup

ice cubes

TO GARNISH

1 pineapple wedge

1 round slice of lime

2 pineapple fronds

drinking straw

paper umbrella (optional)

Place the coconut milk, coconut water, rum, lime juice, frozen pineapple and panela in a high-speed blender and process until puréed. Taste and add more sugar if desired.

Pour into a tall ice-filled glass. Garnish with the pineapple wedge and lime slice, then top off with the pineapple fronds and drinking straw. Add a paper umbrella if you like!

NOTE

Panela is an unrefined cane sugar, typically used in Latin American recipes.

BLOODY MARIA

MAKES 1

60 ml (2 fl oz/¼ cup) blanco tequila

125 ml (4 fl oz/½ cup) tomato juice

2 teaspoons lemon juice

½ teaspoon freshly grated horseradish

½ teaspoon chipotle adobo sauce

½ teaspoon worcestershire sauce

¼ teaspoon hot sauce, or to taste

sea salt and freshly cracked black pepper, to taste

ice cubes

Pickled Taqueria-style vegetables (page 37), to serve on the side

TO GARNISH

1 celery stalk

1 whole pickled jalapeño chilli

2 pickled green beans

Pour the tequila, tomato juice and lemon juice into a jug. Add the horseradish, adobo sauce, worcestershire sauce and hot sauce. Stir to combine, then season with salt and pepper to taste.

Pour into a tall glass filled with ice. Garnish with the celery, pickled chilli and green beans and serve with a side of pickled vegetables.

PINK PALOMA

MAKES 1

1 teaspoon flaked pink Himalayan salt

1 lime wedge

45 ml (1½ fl oz) blanco tequila

60 ml (2 fl oz/¼ cup) ruby red grapefruit juice

60 ml (2 fl oz/¼ cup) soda water (club soda)

15 ml (½ fl oz) agave syrup or Sugar syrup (page 110)

ice cubes

Place the salt on a small plate. Run the lime wedge around the rim of a highball or cocktail glass, then dip the rim into the salt to coat.

Add the tequila, grapefruit juice, soda water and agave syrup to the glass. Stir, add ice, garnish with the lime wedge and serve.

EL DIABLO

MAKES 1

60 ml (2 fl oz/¼ cup) reposado tequila

15 ml (½ fl oz) crème de cassis

15 ml (½ fl oz) lime juice

ice cubes

90 ml (3 fl oz) ginger beer

TO GARNISH

1 lime wedge

2 fresh blackberries

Add the tequila, crème de cassis and lime juice to an ice-filled cocktail shaker and shake for 30 — 45 seconds.

Strain into a tall ice-filled glass, then top up with the ginger beer.

Serve garnished with the lime wedge, and blackberries skewered on a cocktail pick.

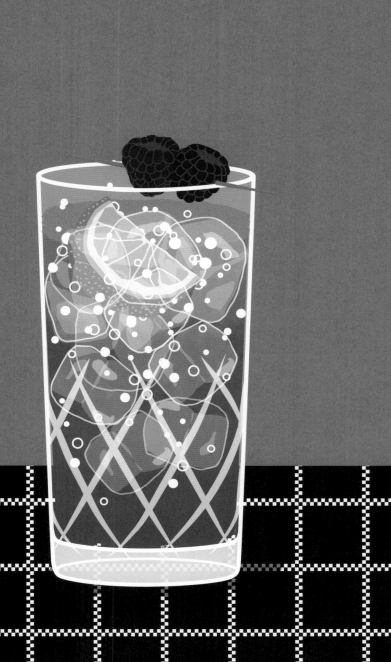

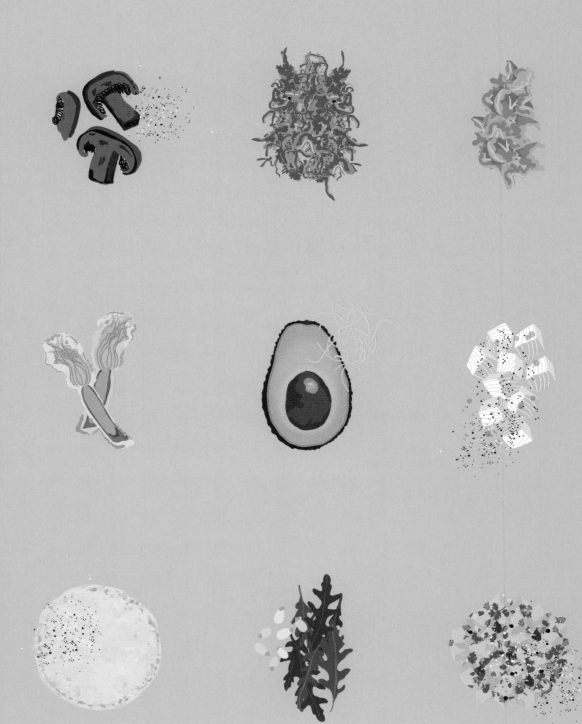

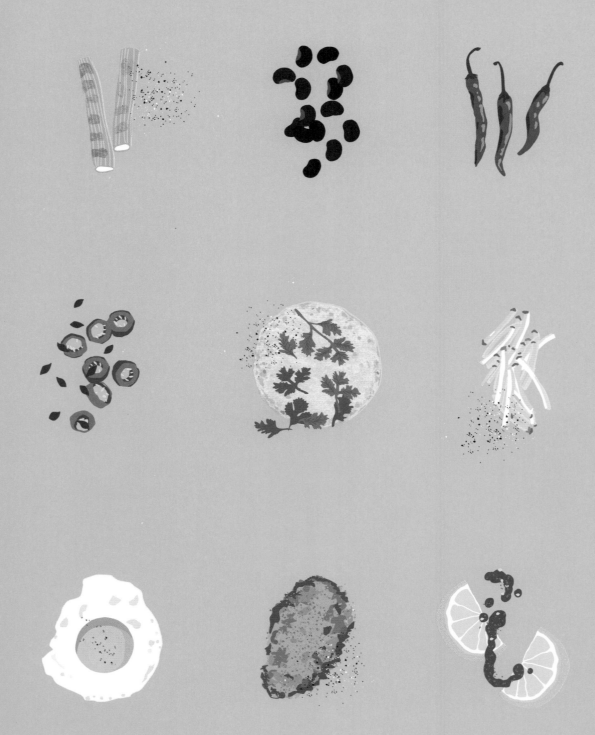

INDEX

VEGAN TACOS
Jackfruit chipotle adobo tacos 40
Turmeric scrambled tofu & spinach tacos 43
Vegan nutty picadillo tacos 44

VEGETARIAN TACOS
Cheesy deep-fried zucchini blossom
    tacos 51
Rajas poblanas & corn tacos 47
Sautéed mushroom & ashed goat's cheese
    tacos 48

FISH TACOS
Baja fish tacos 65
Ceviche Veracruz tacos 61
Spicy ahi poke tacos 57

SEAFOOD TACOS
Chargrilled octopus tacos 62
Lobster tail tacos with lime chilli butter
    54
Oyster po' boy tacos 58

CHICKEN & DUCK TACOS
BBQ spice-rubbed chicken tacos 79
Chicken fajitas tacos 76
Chicken karaage tacos 75
Chicken taquitos 68
Chicken tinga tacos 71
Duck tacos with cherry & blood orange
    salsa 72

PORK TACOS
Carnitas street tacos 82
Chilorio tacos 85
Chorizo, potato & fried egg tacos 86
Pork chilli verde tacos 89
Sweet bahn mi pork belly tacos 90
Yucatán 'cochinita pibil' tacos 93

BEEF TACOS
Beef cheek tacos 103
Beef short ribs 104
Cuban beef picadillo tacos 99
Grilled carne asada tacos 96
Meatball tacos in chipotle adobo 107
Shredded brisket tacos 100

DRINKS
Bloody Maria 122
Coco-loco 121
El diablo 126
Lime, cucumber & chia agua fresca 117
Michelada 114
Pineapple agua fresca 110
Pink paloma 125
Pistachio horchata 118
Watermelon & basil agua fresca 113

BEANS, RICE & QUINOA
Beans in the pot 16
Charro beans 18
Mexican green quinoa 21
Mexican red rice 19
Refried beans 17

TORTILLAS
Corn tortillas 15
Flour tortillas 12

PICKLES
Pickled taqueria-style vegetables 37
Red pickled onion 36

SAUCES
Avocado tomatillo sauce 26
Chilli cooking sauce 103
Chilorio adobo sauce 85
Chipotle adobo sauce 107
Chipotle crema 104
Green chilli sauce 33
Habanero hot sauce 28
Lime chilli butter 54
Red chilli sauce 32
Roasted tomato cooking sauce 93
Spicy remoulade sauce 58
Sriracha crema 57
Tinga sauce 71
Vegan lime coriander crema 40
Verde sauce 89

SALSAS
Cherry & blood orange salsa 72
Guacamole 34
Mango salsa 26
Pico de gallo 34
Pineapple salsa 31
Red tomato salsa 29
Roasted corn & black bean salsa 25
Roasted tomato salsa 30
Tomatillo salsa verde 24

MARINADES
Achiote marinade 93
Lemon, chilli & garlic marinade 62
Lime, coriander & chilli marinade 76
Lime, lemon & chipotle marinade 96
Shoyu & ginger marinade 57
Tamari & ginger marinade 75

TOPPINGS & SLAWS
Chicharrones 20
Coriander slaw 65
Dukkah 48
Quick pickle cabbage slaw 90
Spicy slaw 75

Smith Street Books

Published in 2018 by Smith Street Books
Collingwood | Melbourne | Australia
smithstreetbooks.com

ISBN: 978-1-925418-81-1

Copyright recipes & text © Smith Street Books
Copyright design © Smith Street Books
Copyright illustrations © Alice Oehr

CIP data is available from the National
Library of Australia

Publisher: Paul McNally
Design & art direction: Michelle Mackintosh
Recipes: Deborah Kaloper
Illustrations: Alice Oehr
Layout: Heather Menzies, Studio31 Graphics
Editor: Katri Hilden

Printed & bound in China by C&C Offset
Printing Co., Ltd.

Book 62
10 9 8 7 6 5 4 3 2 1

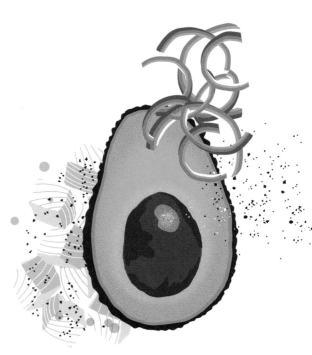

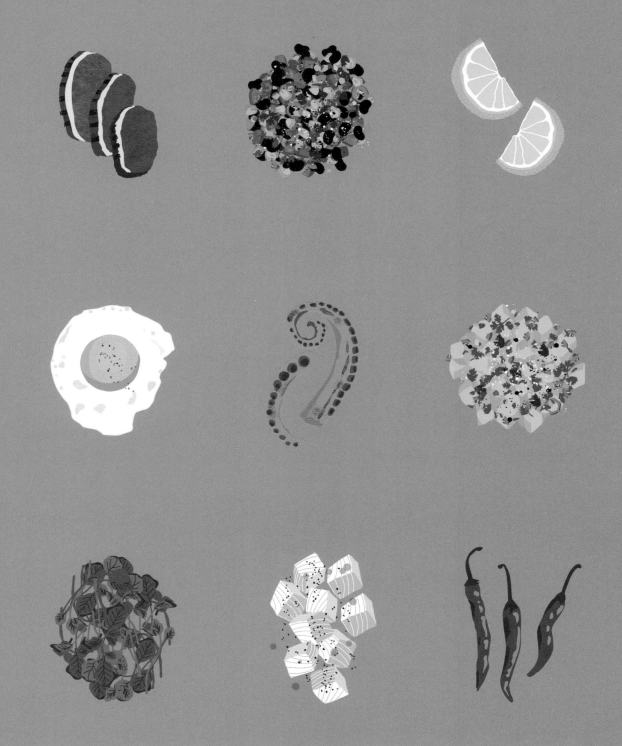

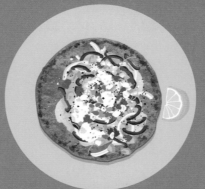

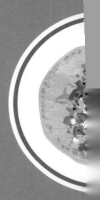
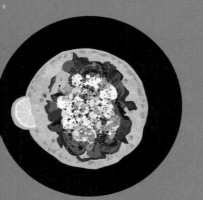
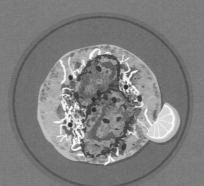